THE MISSIONARY MANIFESTO

THE MISSIONARY MANIFESTO

BY

G. CAMPBELL MORGAN

Wipf and Stock Publishers
199 W 8th Ave, Suite 3
Eugene, OR 97401

The Missionary Manifesto
By Morgan, G. Campbell
ISBN: 1-59752-671-1
Publication date 5/4/2006
Previously published by Hodder and Stoughton, 1909

TO

JOHN GREGORY MANTLE,

TO WHOSE FRIENDSHIP AND INTERPRETATION,

I OWE MORE THAN I CAN EVER TELL

FOR MISSIONARY INTEREST AND

INSPIRATION, I DEDICATE

THESE LECTURES.

CONTENTS

THE FOURFOLD COMMISSION

"*And Jesus came to them and spake unto them, saying, All authority hath been given unto Me in heaven and on earth. Go ye therefore, and disciple the nations, baptizing them into the name of the Father and of the Son and of the Holy Ghost: teaching them to observe all things whatsoever I commanded you: and lo, I am with you all the days, even unto the consummation of the age.*"—MATTHEW xxviii. 18–20.

"*And He said unto them, Go ye into all the kosmos and preach the gospel to the whole creation. He that believeth and is baptized shall be saved; but he that disbelieveth shall be condemned.*"—MARK xvi. 15, 16.

"*Ye are witnesses of these things. And behold, I send forth the promise of My Father upon you: but tarry ye in the city, until ye be clothed with power from on high.*"—LUKE xxiv. 48, 49.

"*Jesus therefore said to them again, Peace be unto you: as the Father hath sent Me, even so send I you. And when He had said this, He breathed on them, and saith unto them, Receive ye the Holy Ghost: whose soever sins ye forgive, they are forgiven unto them; whose soever sins ye retain, they are retained.*"—JOHN xx. 21–23.

I

THE FOURFOLD COMMISSION

ANY one reading these passages of Scripture for the first time would certainly be quite as much impressed by their disparities as by their similarities.

It is the custom of the Christian Church to speak of the commission of Jesus, as though there were but one, which the four evangelists record in different words. This conception is the result of superficial observation, and the measure in which it dominates our thinking is the measure in which we fail to recognise the spaciousness and inclusiveness of the missionary commission, and fail therefore to understand the real responsibility of the Church.

On the other hand, there are those who,

recognising the differences between the records of the evangelists, affirm that they contradict each other.

In order to avoid these two mistakes—that on the one hand of imagining that we have four reports of one commission in different words; and that on the other hand of imagining that the four contradict each other—it is important that we should recognise the true nature of these Gospel narratives. I am growingly convinced that the measure in which we recognise the humanity of them, is the measure in which we shall be driven to the conclusion that they are infinitely more than human. To come to a study of them with a foregone and mechanical conception of inspiration is to miss the music of their harmony, and to fail to discover the ultimate meaning of their message.

These Gospels are the narratives of four men, of different temperament, and consequently of different outlook. They are the natural, simple, and truthful accounts of things which they either saw and heard themselves, or learned from eye-witnesses. In these stories then, we gather the impressions which were made upon these different men by the Person of Christ, and by His teaching.

This is equally true of the records of the happenings after the resurrection, as of the account of events in the life and ministry of Jesus, which culminated in the Cross. All the evangelists tell the story of the death and resurrection of Jesus. Moreover, they all give some account of the events happening subsequently to resurrection. Neither of them gives a detailed account of all that Jesus did or said in the forty days that passed between His resurrection and ascension. They rather describe with perfect naturalness those doings of Jesus, or record with simple accuracy those of His words, which impressed them. They looked upon Him, and listened to Him in the upper room in Jerusalem, on the highways where they walked with Him, on the slopes of Olivet, or on the shores of the lake; or they heard the account of these things from those who did so look and listen to Him. Each man was impressed by things which Jesus did and said according to his natural temperament.

This is perfectly natural, and is illustrated by the fact that it is always true that having listened to the address of a teacher, or the sermon of a preacher, any company of men, gathering together afterwards to discuss the message would find that different parts of the address would have impressed each man, largely according to his temperament or need.

Recognising this fact, we begin to understand these Gospel narratives. The harmony of result proves the Divine over-ruling and choice of instruments. The choosing of each of the evangelists for the writing of the story was the choosing of the Spirit; and the principle of choice was the necessity for recording and retaining, for the coming centuries, the very things which each man would naturally write.

Thus to begin on the human level is to be driven to the conclusion of the Divinity of these narratives. When we understand that these are perfectly simple and artless stories, written by men who had no conception that they were inspired; and when we review the whole, and discover how part fits to part, and how each revelation complements the others, until the four merge into the perfect presentation of a perfect Person, then we see that these men; who wrote truthfully, simply, and artlessly, on human levels; were guided, directed, inspired, by one Master-mind for the revelation to all time of great and sufficient truth.

If that be true of the whole Book, it is certainly true of the commission of Jesus. The complete manifesto of missionary enterprise is not contained in any one Gospel. If we would know what the missionary responsibility of the Church really is, it is not enough to read what Matthew has written. We must also read what Mark records, what Luke reports, and what John reveals. We must gather the whole manifesto from the harmony of these Gospel revelations.

In this introductory chapter I propose in barest outline to consider the whole commission. In succeeding chapters I shall take the separate parts thereof, as reported in the four Gospels, and consider each carefully; finally dealing with the resources and consequent responsibilities thus revealed.

Before the harmony of the Missionary Commission can be appreciated, the harmony of the Gospels in their presentation of the Person of the Christ must be recognised. We have all at some time either purchased a harmony of the Gospels, or attempted to arrange these stories in chronological order. The result of our purchase, or our labour, has been unsatisfactory. In such labour I personally discovered the impossibility of the task. It is well to remember, moreover, that when a chronological harmony of the Gospels is attempted, the one so attempting is in grave peril of destroying the spiritual harmony. This spiritual harmony consists in the presentation of the Person of the Christ in a fourfold aspect.

In the Gospel according to Matthew the Kingship of Jesus is revealed. It is impossible to escape from that impression. It is the Gospel of His authority: authority by all rights—the rights of inherent royalty as revealed in His character; the right of perfect legislation, as indicated in His manifesto; the right of victorious administration, which includes conflict, and issues in victory as accomplished through His Cross and Resurrection. Matthew closes his Gospel with a picture of this King, standing in the power of resurrection, and saying with quiet dignity "All authority hath been given unto Me." Matthew's Gospel is supremely that of the royalty of Jesus.

The Gospel according to Mark is the Gospel of the service of Jesus. He is seen therein perpetually stripped of royal apparel, and girded "with the slave's apron"; for evermore at work in remarkable and victorious power. As we watch Him at His work, we see the aims of His activity—the destruction of the destroyer, the casting out of demons, the cancelling of disease. But His work is constructive also: He makes again those who had been destroyed; He flings out death and gives back life; He cures disease, and thus restores men to ability. Through all these processes He is seen restoring groaning creation; destroying things that destroy, in order that those destroyed might be restored; in order that man, and all beneath Him, might be healed and helped. It is the Gospel of the Servant of God, mighty in power, working without cessation even to the point of weariness, until He crowns service in actual and absolute sacrifice. Mark presents the Servant, and closes his Gospel with the statement that the Lord works with those who go into Creation with His evangel of renewal.

The perfect humanity of Jesus is portrayed in Luke's Gospel. As Luke, the master-artist, the cultured Greek, proceeds with his work, we see in Jesus the realisation of the Divine purpose; a perfect personality. He records the development of the early years—the birth of the Boy; the mental awakening, and the confirmation at twelve years of age; the spiritual crowning of the Man at thirty years of age. We then see this perfect Man, passing through the three years of public ministry, victorious through testing; submitting to temptation, but mastering it; walking the common way of ordinary human life, yet never failing, never deviating; moving straight forward with calm strength and dignity through all opposing forces to the realisation of His own human life. We see finally, not merely the victory of personality but the accomplishment of vocation. This perfect Person, victorious in His own probation, has a mission. "The Son of Man came to seek and to save that which was lost." And ere the Gospel close, we see Him accomplishing His Passion, rising from the dead, promising the gift of the Holy Spirit, and ascending to the right hand of the Father. Luke records the command of Jesus that His disciples should be witnesses to His victory in the power of the Spirit.

Turning to the last Gospel, we are conscious of the clouds and darkness of a great mystery; yet out of it there flashes such light as man had never seen before. The Gospel of John is not a life of Jesus. It is an orderly and sequential setting forth of certain words and works that reveal the deepest mystery of His Being. We see in Him the manifestation of Deity. In His Being, we come to a knowledge of the Being of God. In His sayings, we learn the truth of God. In His doings, we discover the activities of God. John records the sublime words in which Jesus sent His disciples forth for the continuation of that ministry for which He was the Sent of God.

So these men wrote. Matthew, the tax-gatherer, living in the midst of things imperial, saw the King and described Him. Mark, the friend of Peter, a fisherman accustomed to the long vigil of the night and the ceaseless toil of the day, wrote of the Man at work. Luke, the Greek physician, individual perfection being the master idea of his mental outlook, saw the fulfilment of that ideal in Jesus. John, the mystic dreamer of the Galilean sea, looking ever on, and looking through to the ultimate, saw the "Word made flesh."

In the light of that fourfold revelation we discover the harmony of the missionary commission.

Matthew, who portrayed the royalty of Jesus, was supremely impressed with Christ's words on the slopes of Olivet. "All authority hath been given unto Me in heaven and on earth. Go ye therefore, and make disciples of all the nations, baptizing them into the name of the Father and of the Son and of the Holy Ghost; teaching them to observe all things whatsoever I commanded you."

"Go ye, . . . disciple the nations," is a much broader commission than that indicated by the translation, "Go, make disciples of the nations." The individual application is recognised in the following words, "baptizing them," that is, those who obey the proclamation of royalty by submission; "teaching them," that is, the bringing of such under His ethical system. "Go . . . disciple . . . teach." This is the commission of the King, the Law-giver. It rings with the note of authority.

The commission according to Mark is all too superficially read and considered by Christian people. "Go ye into all the kosmos" does not merely mean, Travel over the surface of the earth and speak to men; the term "kosmos" here includes man and everything beneath him. "The preaching of the gospel to individual men is the beginning of the work, but the gospel is to be proclaimed to the whole creation. He can only reach the kosmos and the whole creation with the evangel through men. In the proportion in which men hear the evangel, and, yielding to it, are remade by the healing ministry of the Servant of God, they become instruments through which He is able to reconstruct the order of the whole creation.

Take the simplest illustration. In the Welsh revival, when a profane, degraded, brutalised collier, brought to God, went next morning to the mines to begin his day's work, he found himself unable to induce his horse to work, because he no longer swore or ill-treated the animal, which only understood profane language and only answered brutal blows.

Through the renewed man the whole creation is affected and redeemed as it passes under the dominion of love. We are to go into the whole creation, the whole kosmos, and to preach the evangel, not merely to men and women, though that is first and fundamental, but through them to the whole creation.

This Servant of God comes into human life, and wherever it is limited and bruised He destroys the destroyer. The work of His people is that of carrying on His work. They must speak with the commanding note of authority; but there must also be that sacrificial service which enters into the life of the world, and comes into contact with the suffering, in order that there may be infused thereinto the healing virtues of the Lord Jesus Christ Himself.

Luke, the writer of the Gospel of the perfect Manhood of Christ, records His declaration. "Ye are witnesses of these things . . . but tarry ye . . . until ye be clothed with power from on high." Christ was victorious in life and death, and we are to vindicate His victory by repeating it in our lives, and manifesting to men the fact that the power of His life and the value of His death are at their disposal. We are to be witnesses.

John heard the mystic words that the others perchance were afraid to chronicle, because they so little understood their meaning. "As the Father hath sent Me, even so send I you. . . . Receive ye the Holy Ghost: whose soever sins ye forgive, they are forgiven unto them; whose soever sins ye retain, they are retained." John, who had seen the gleaming glory of Divine light shining through the love-lit eyes of his Master; John, who had heard in the sweet tones of his Master's voice the very music of the infinite and undying Love, now heard Him say, "As the Father hath sent Me, even so send I you." As He came into the world for the manifestation of God, He sends His own into the world for that manifestation. As that manifestation of God included the work whereby sin may be forgiven, we are to go in the power of all He has accomplished and are to exercise this great and holy function of remitting and retaining sins. This word was spoken, not to the apostles as such, but to Christian men and women. They are all called to reveal the Father to men, and to exercise the right of the remission or retention of sins.

It is as we discover the distinctions between these records that we also discover the harmony of the commission. Each is related to the Person of Christ, and each emphasises one supreme value thereof. The King sends us to proclaim His royalty. The

Servant calls us to co-operation in His sacrificial service. The Perfect Man calls us to demonstrate the possibility of perfection through His victory won in our lives. God manifest, sends us forth to exhibit "the excellencies of Him" Who has called us "out of darkness into His marvellous light."

We may now approach the subject from another standpoint, that of the harmony of these commissions as related to the needs of the world.

The need of humanity to-day is fourfold. Its first necessity is that of authority. That is true in many directions. I now make one application only. Humanity pre-eminently needs to hear the voice of authority on the matter of moral standards. To turn away from the religion of the Lord Christ, and to study the philosophies of men is to discover a great disagreement on the question of sin. There is no final authority on this subject. Therefore the supreme need of the world is the enunciation of an ethic which is binding and authoritative, and which therefore gives a clear revelation of what sin is.

The first note of the Christian commission

is the proclamation to the world of the authority of Jesus. The Lordship of Christ should be the first note of preaching, whether at home or abroad. We wrongly imagine that our first duty is to declare His love, and the fact that He is able to save. It may be an old-fashioned doctrine, but it is one to which we need to return, that man never enters into the experience of conversion until he has come to conviction of need. That conviction of need, which is conviction of sin, can only be produced by an authoritative moral standard. That standard is provided in the ethic of Jesus, proclaimed in His teaching, and exemplified in His life.

If the first note of the world's need is that of authority, the next is that of the universal consciousness of sorrow and pain. These two matters are not related in the thinking of man to-day as they should be. Man wants to know what is right and what is wrong, and cannot find his final standard. He is also conscious of sorrow, of pain; and that pain is felt through all the life that lies beneath him in creation. He fails too often to recognise that the pain results from the violation of law, through lack of submission to a final authority. When the nature-poet found a dead robin on his garden path, he said—

> "Our human touch had on him passed,
> And with our touch, our agony";

and the whole truth is expressed in the pulsating, throbbing words of the great apostle, "the whole creation groaneth and travaileth in pain together until now." Humanity needs healing in order to the healing of creation.

The second note of the great evangel is that of the carrying to the whole creation the message of healing and renewal. The world's agony is the world's need. That need is to be met by the disciples of Christ, as they enter the creation which groaneth and travaileth in pain, in sacrificial service, through which the destructive forces are to be destroyed and new life communicated.

The third note in the world's need is its consciousness of inability to realise the highest, to do the noblest, to be the best. In the presence of that inability men think differently, and act in various ways. Some deny the ideal, because they are unable to realise it. This need, stripped of all false arguments and philosophies, may be expressed in the language of Paul, "To me who would do good, evil is present."

The third note in the commission is, "Ye shall be My witnesses." The disciples of Jesus are to go through the world demonstrating Christ's ability in their victorious lives. They are to be His witnesses, the men and women who are able. Paul also said, "I can do all things in Him that strengtheneth me." Those submitted to His royalty, who know the healing power He bestows, in whom the forces that destroy are destroyed, are to be witnesses to Him, in the home, in the city, in shop and office and factory, and to the uttermost part of the earth. Wherever they go they are to be credentials, evidences, demonstrations, proofs, samples of Christ, answering the world's wail of inability with their perpetual song of ability.

The final note of the world's need is expressed in the universal unrest, that surging under-current of unexplained dissatisfaction which characterises humanity everywhere. Probe it, solve it, and it will be discovered that it is all the outcome of the fact that humanity is out of harmony with God. One cannot turn in any direction without being made conscious of unrest and fear and suspicion; instability in government, wickedness in diplomacy, the breaking of treaties; all the things of unrest are parts of the same lack of God. The sins of men result from the sin of man wherein he turned from God. For the forgiveness of sins men need reconciliation to God.

The last note of the commission is, "As the Father hath sent Me, even so send I you"; with its necessary sequence, "whose soever sins ye forgive, they are forgiven unto them; whose soever sins ye retain, they are retained." In the mystic power of her fellowship with Christ, the Church is sent to reveal the Father, to work together with the Father in order that the world may find its rest where it alone can be found, in restored fellowship with Him by the putting away of sins.

Finally, let us note the harmony of results following obedience to the whole commission.

The immediate result of the proclamation of the royalty of Jesus is conviction of sin.

The immediate result of the proclamation of His evangel to the creation, in the power of sacrificial service, is that of a conviction of the possibility of righteousness. That possibility is demonstrated by the healing of humanity's wounds, the ending of sorrow, the putting away of pain and the communication of power.

The immediate result of witnessing to the power of Christ among the nations is that of the conviction of judgment, because the prince of this world hath been judged. A Christian man, living the strong, pure Christian life, is an evidence of the fact that the forces of evil are mastered, and that all who obey the Evangel may be victorious over them.

The immediate result of conveying to the

world the great revelation of the Father and the message of the forgiveness of sins, is that of the creation of a belief which becomes the basis of that repentance which is the rock foundation on which character is built and human life developed.

This then, is the full manifesto of the King concerning the responsibility of His Church.

She is sent to the waiting world to proclaim His royalty.

She is called to serve with Him in suffering, in order that she may communicate healing to the whole creation.

She is to prove her Master's power to realise in men the highest and the noblest, by the transfigured lives of her members.

She is to reveal the Father, in the mystery of that Passion, whereby sin is remitted when men yield to his claim, or retained when they persist in rebellion against Him.

These are the values for which the world is waiting. The authority of the King must be the first note in all the Church's preaching. She must never lower the standards of His ethical requirement, nor remain passive when others do so. Moreover, she must ever press on through all cities and countries and continents proclaiming His will. By its own inherent truth His teaching will appeal to the hearts and consciences of men when it is preached. In His words the world will find the final laws of conduct, and in Himself the final standard of character.

But the Church must also strip herself of her purple, and array herself in the garments of service, girding herself with humility as with a slave's apron. Passing into the midst of creation's sigh and sob and sorrow, its wounds and weariness, she must touch it with new life, healing by contact. She is to bring to that world-agony, which results from the fact that the world has lost its centre of authority, the answering agony of sacrificial service by which, and by which alone, it can be healed.

The Church is to scatter through all the nations the living witnesses. The groaning creation is "Waiting for the revealing of the sons of God." That word, though prophetic, has an immediate and present application. Wherever those come, in whom Christ has won His victory, by their lives they preach in power the gospel of His ability.

Finally, the Church is to go with the great message of the forgiveness of sins. The man who is brought face to face with the royalty of Jesus will put his hand upon his lip and cry, "Unclean! Unclean!" He will thus become conscious of all the sorrow and pain resulting from his sin. He will then know as never before the agony of inability to do that which he would. To such the Church must declare the possibility of the forgiveness of sins by the unveiling of the Father.

This is the Church's deposit. If she rejoice in all that she possesses of authority, of service, of witness, and of revelation; and fail to communicate to others, she is untrue to the intention of her Lord, and is in grave peril herself of losing all.

THE COMMISSION ACCORDING TO MATTHEW

"Go ye therefore, and disciple the nations, baptizing them into the name of the Father and of the Son and of the Holy Ghost: teaching them to observe all things whatsoever I commanded you: and lo, I am with you all the days, even unto the consummation of the age."—MATTHEW xxviii. 19, 20.

II

THE AUTHORITY OF THE KING

THERE is a common method in the presentation of the four parts of the Missionary Manifesto by the four evangelists. An aspect of truth which the commission emphasises is stated; the responsibility of the Church concerning that aspect is declared; and the power in which the Church may discharge her responsibility is revealed.

In our consideration of the Manifesto in its four aspects, we shall observe this method in each case by attempting to discover the deposit, the debt, and the dynamic.

The words "deposit" and "debt" are closely allied in any consideration of the Church's missionary responsibility. Paul, in writing to the Romans, said: "I am debtor both to Greeks and to barbarians, both to the wise and to the foolish." We may understand what he meant by the declaration by reference to his second letter to Timothy, in which he said: "I know Him Whom I have believed, and I am persuaded that He is able to guard that which I have committed unto Him against that day." This passage, as it thus stands in the Revised Version, or as it reads in the Authorised, "I know Him Whom I have believed, and am persuaded that He is able to keep that which I have committed unto Him against that day," is more than translation; it is interpretation. The phrase "that which I have committed unto Him," common to both versions, is the equivalent to something much briefer in the Greek New Testament, which literally translated reads "my deposit." Such translation would leave the question open as to whether the apostle referred to something he had deposited with Christ, or to something which Christ had deposited with him. I submit that the decision must be made by an examination of the context. In this last letter to Timothy Paul was urging him not to be ashamed of the testimony of the Lord, and in the course of the paragraph referred to the gospel of which he had been appointed a preacher, apostle, and teacher; and declared that he himself was not ashamed because he knew Him Whom he had believed, and was persuaded that He was able to guard his deposit. The deposit was evidently the gospel.

In the Roman letter, in close connection with his declaration that he was debtor, he made the same declaration, "I am not ashamed of the gospel." His deposit thus created his debt. That deposit was the gospel which he held in trust for the world. That the responsibility was a grave one he knew full well, and in yet another letter, when speaking of the difficulties of the work of the Christian ministry, he exclaimed, "Who is sufficient for these things?" and, in close association with the inquiry, affirmed, "Our sufficiency is of God."

Thus, in the Manifesto of Jesus, we shall find the gospel for the world, which is the Church's deposit; a responsibility, which is the Church's debt; and the revelation of the power in which the debt may be discharged, which is the Church's dynamic.

In Matthew the revelation of Jesus is that of the perfect and all-sufficient King. Consequently, and naturally, when he wrote the story of the resurrection and the events following it, he only referred to those words of Jesus which grew distinctly and emphatically out of His Kingship. All that Matthew had to tell concerning the resurrection and the subsequent occurrences is chronicled in the last chapter of his Gospel. So far as the actual resurrection is concerned, everything is told in the first ten verses. Immediately following that is a passage which we may treat as a parenthesis, in which he gave an account of the going of the guard into the city, and of the way in which the priests promised to shield them in case of Pilate's anger. In the last few verses we have the account of the meeting in Galilee. It must be remembered that this meeting was not on the day of resurrection, but long subsequent thereto, and therefore the commission which Matthew gives was uttered by the Lord subsequently to those recorded by Mark, Luke, and John. According to Matthew, He said to the women on the resurrection morning; "Fear not; go tell My brethren that they depart into Galilee, and there shall they see Me." He gives no account of further happenings on that first day, and we read; "But the eleven went into Galilee, unto the mountain where Jesus had appointed them." That could not have happened on the same day. There is evidently a gap in the story. The distance between Jerusalem and Galilee was more than fifty miles. Mark, Luke, and John, in each case with particular emphasis and careful indication of time, affirm that on the evening of the day of resurrection He met the disciples in the upper room where they were assembled. Moreover, it is evident, from careful comparison of the narratives, that on the afternoon of the day of resurrection He walked to Emmaus with two disciples, and appeared subsequently to the eleven assembled in the upper room. Chronologically therefore, it is evident that the charge given to the disciples in Galilee must be placed later than the instructions given to them in the upper room, as recorded by Mark, Luke, and John. I nevertheless believe that both the gospel and the note of the commission according to Matthew are found in their true place in the New Testament, because the first note of the Church's message to the world must ever be that of the Lordship of Christ. Yet let us not forget that this is only one note. To make this the one inclusive charge of Christ to His disciples is to fail to apprehend the full and spacious meaning of missionary endeavour.

In order to the clearest apprehension of the value of the words of Jesus uttered in Galilee, let us particularly notice some of the facts which Matthew records concerning the meeting of the King with His disciples on that occasion. "The eleven disciples went into Galilee, unto the mountain where Jesus had appointed them. And when they saw Him, they worshipped Him; but some doubted. And Jesus came to them and spake unto them." It is interesting to notice the effect that was produced upon these men by the appearance of Jesus. There are suggestions concerning that appearance which it may not be possible finally to explain, but the inference of the declaration, "Jesus came to them," is that when they first saw Him, He was at some distance from them, perhaps standing a little higher on the mountain side. As they looked at Him they worshipped; but some doubted; and the suggestion is that there was something in His appearance which compelled them to this attitude of worship. The word "worship" here used means absolute prostration in the presence of supremacy and sovereignty. In different forms it occurs about twelve times in the course of this Gospel, and about twelve times in the course of the Gospel according to John. It is practically absent from those of Mark and Luke. These things are not accidents in the economy of inspired revelation. In the Gospel which presents the King, and in that which demonstrates Deity, that attitude is referred to repeatedly. In those presenting Jesus as Servant and as Man the word is almost entirely absent.

While this word occurs over and over again in Matthew, here at Galilee it gains a new significance, which is accentuated by the declaration that "some doubted."

"When they saw Him they worshipped Him." There was evidently something about His appearance which commanded the attitude of worship, which bent these men before Him in submission and adoration. What the peculiar nature of the appearance was, of course it is impossible to declare, but my own conviction is that its effect upon them was due to the fact that He was "declared to be the Son of God with power, according to the Spirit of holiness, by the resurrection of the dead." With reverent reticence Matthew gives us no description of the appearance. He affirms that "when they saw Him, they worshipped Him." The declaration "but some doubted" is a valuable evidence of the truth of the story. Were this narrative a human fabrication it is not likely that these words would have been written. The word "doubted" is an uncommon one, only occurring twice in the New Testament, and each occurrence is in this Gospel. Peter walked on the water to go to his Lord, and when he looked at the boisterous waves he was afraid, doubted, wavered. Other words translated "doubt" in the New Testament suggest unbelief. This one indicates wavering, wondering, perplexity. In the hearts of some of them there still lurked fear and uncertainty. They had seen Him die. They had been gathered about Him in the upper room on more than one occasion. He had appeared to one and another of them, and to the whole company assembled together. They were sure that He had risen. When they saw Him on the slopes of Olivet there was something in His appearance which demanded worship; and yet they could hardly believe their senses—their minds wavered. It is to be remembered that no word of rebuke fell from the lips of Christ. He came nearer to them, and perchance by that coming, banished for ever the fears that had lingered in their hearts, making impossible in all the days to come any further doubt. The scene then is before our minds. The risen and glorified Lord stands in the midst of the group of worshipping men, some of them wavering in fear born of wonder. To them He uttered the words of His Kingly commission, in which we may discover the deposit of truth for which the Church is responsible, the debt created by the possession of that deposit, and the dynamic in the power of which the Church may discharge the debt created by the possession of the deposit.

The deposit is named in the claim of Christ; "All authority hath been given unto Me in heaven and on earth." The debt is declared in the command of Christ; "Go ye therefore, and disciple the nations, baptizing them into the name of the Father and of the Son and of the Holy Ghost." The dynamic is revealed in the promise of Christ; "Lo, I am with you all the days, even unto the consummation of the age."

First then, the deposit of the Church. The one truth emphasised in this phase of the Missionary Manifesto is that of the absolute authority of Christ; His supremacy and sovereignty; the fact that He shares the throne of empire with none. The word here translated "authority" does not suggest power in the sense of energy or might.

The first intention of the word is that of the power of choice—that is, the right to choose. Its second intention is that of the power of enforcement—that is, the right to insist upon obedience. The third intention is that of the power of government—that is, the right to utter the final verdict and to pass sentence.

Human choice must always be made in submission to a higher will, therefore it can never be said that man can have an absolute right and power of choice. Authority in the last analysis is the right to determine, enforce, and pass sentence.

In these words Jesus, standing on the resurrection side of His grave, in the simplest language made the sublimest claim, when He thus declared Himself to be King by Divine right, and therefore absolute in His Kingship. The word admits of no qualification. The claim admits of no limitation. In that moment He claimed authority in the material, mental, and moral realms.

The application of His claim to this world does by no means exhaust it. He swept the compass with a reach far wider, more spacious, and stupendous. Not only on earth, but in heaven is authority given to Him. The one phrase, "in heaven and on earth," includes the whole creation of God. It is manifest that He is excluded Who created, and Who puts all things under the feet of His King. It is equally manifest that all is included which comes within the scope of that comprehensive word, the creation of God. We may interpret this final claim of Jesus by the prayer He taught His disciples; "Our Father Who art in the heavens. Hallowed be Thy name. Thy Kingdom come. Thy will be done, as in heaven, so on earth." His ministry of teaching having been completed, having accomplished His exodus and resurrection, at last He claimed authority in heaven and on earth, thus assuming the throne of empire over the whole creation of God, included in the terms of the prayer, and now defined in the words, "in heaven and on earth."

Of course, this is but to state the fact in the broadest and most comprehensive way. To those who will give themselves to careful consideration of it, there will come an ever-increasing consciousness of the grandeur and sublimity of the claim. This authority moreover, is the more remarkable in that Jesus described it as delegated authority. Ultimately, it is the authority of essential Deity.

Perhaps we come nearest to an understanding of the special value of these words of Jesus when we consider what they meant to the men who first heard them. To them the claim must have been that of the vindication of the ideals for which He had stood through the years of His public ministry; the ratification of the purposes which He had declared to them in the process of His patient training of them for the work which they were called to do; and consequently it suggested the initiation of the new era of their new responsibility.

One recognises the difficulty of speaking of the ideals of Jesus with anything like brevity, and yet it is necessary to make the attempt. For the purpose of a study such as this, the master principles upon which He had insisted both in His speech and manner of life through the years of

His public ministry; in the more pronounced discourses which fell from His lips, in all His arguments with His critics, and in the private teaching of His disciples; may be stated as the supremacy of the spiritual, and the necessity for heart purity. Again, out of the mass of His teaching it is difficult to cite a lonely illustration of the fact that He stood for the supremacy of the spiritual. Perhaps one of the simplest is that conveyed in His words; "Be not afraid of them which kill the body, but are not able to kill the soul." Here is a distinct recognition of the fact that the essential life of a man is independent of the body. The man of the world would affirm that to kill the body is to kill the life; consequently the only thing he fears is the death of the body, and for evermore he strives to deliver his body from death, because he sees nothing beyond its destruction. Jesus, with a fine disdain for that which is merely physical, in these words indicated His conception that the supreme thing in human life is not the physical but the spiritual. At last, upon the slopes of Olivet, He stood in the glory of a life that vindicates the word spoken before death. He went to the Cross not fearing those who kill the body but could not destroy the life. He knew, that although they nailed Him to the tree, they could not hinder Him, or hurt Him in the deepest facts of His being. Now in resurrection life He said; "All authority hath been given unto Me, in heaven and on earth," and a fair application of His words may be, I have vindicated the ideal for which I stood, that namely, of the supremacy of the spiritual.

He stood moreover, for the necessity of purity in the inward part, for evermore condemning, not so much the outward action as the inward desire. According to the testimony of her accusers, a woman was taken in the act, and arraigned before Him; but He was far more shocked by the unmanifested lust of the men who charged her, than by the story of her sin. In all His teaching He had made it clear that what a man is in his deepest life is what he is in very truth in the sight of Heaven, in the balances of eternity, in the conception of

God. This Man, Himself a Man of inward purity and heart spotlessness, went to death, and, in virtue of that purity, did what no other had done — He mastered death. Because He was sinless He gained the victory over death. The disciples heard Him say; "All authority hath been given unto Me, in heaven and on earth," and knew in their deepest consciousness that His resurrection was the vindication of His own claim to sinlessness; and the vindication therefore, of His ideal of the necessity for heart purity.

These are the ideals He has committed to His Church, to which she must yield a ready submission within her own borders, and which she is called upon to proclaim with no uncertain sound to all the nations.

His claim to authority meant also a declaration of the ratification of His purposes. He had told His disciples that He would build His Church; that He would lead it as an army in conflict against evil and its issues, and in victory over all, including the very gates of Hades; that He would erect a moral standard, and make them, His disciples, His interpreters thereof, giving them "the keys of the Kingdom of heaven."

Immediately following this declaration of purpose, He had spoken to them of the necessity for the Cross, and they, with faith faltering, had seen Him die. Notwithstanding all He had foretold them, they looked upon the Cross as evidence of His failure to accomplish His purposes. From their standpoint of observation it was impossible for one who died to build a Church, and lead an army, and insist upon a moral standard. But now they saw Him in all the glory of resurrection life, and knew that therein He demonstrated His power to build a Church, having passed through death and become the firstborn from among the dead. They knew that He had the power to combat sin and overcome it, for He had taken hold of death, which is the ultimate of sin, and in His mastery of death had revealed His ability to deal with sin. He had lived in perfect conformity to His own ethical standard, and when His life resulted in His rejection by men and His being put to death, it had seemed as though the impossibility of obedience was proven; but now, standing in the power of risen life, He claimed authority; and thereby suggested that His own victories vindicated His right to be the ethical Teacher of the world.

Not only did that claim, emphasised by the resurrection, vindicate His ideals and ratify His purposes, it declared that the hour had come for the initiation of the mission of seeking and saving the lost.

That absolute Lordship is the first message which the Church is charged to deliver to the world, and the supreme proof of it is the resurrection. I am not prepared to declare that we are wronging the Lord Christ when we emphasise His Lordship upon the basis of the perfection of His example. I do however say that the preaching of His example will never subdue sinning men to His Lordship. I do not affirm that it is wholly inaccurate to declare that in the high conceptions of life revealed in His ethical teaching is reason for crowning Him. I do however affirm that we may preach His ethic without being able to win victories in the moral realm. The Church's message is not fundamentally that He is Lord by reason of the matchless beauty of His own life, or on account of the lonely splendour of His moral standard. The Church is called to declare that He is Lord by the resurrection of the dead. To deny the historic truth of the resurrection is to blot out every missionary commission in the New Testament. If in answer it be affirmed that He commissioned His disciples to certain work before His Cross and resurrection, in reply we have only to examine the earlier commissions. In the earlier days of His ministry, He said among other things; "Go not into any way of the Gentiles, and enter not into any city of the Samaritans." Beyond the resurrection His charge was no longer local, but universal, the whole creation being included. The first business of the Church is to proclaim to the world the authority of the King Who came to empire by the way of resurrection.

If that be the deposit, what then, is the debt? It is clearly indicated as to its widest scope in the words "disciple the nations." The Church's responsibility as indicated by these words is that of the proclamation of the Lordship of Christ, the insistence upon the supremacy of His ethic in every nation, among all peoples. His messengers are charged to proclaim the fact of His Lordship, to announce to men everywhere that He is King. They are to pass through all nations proclaiming Him King upon the basis of His resurrection, and all that it involves. This means therefore, that she is to proclaim and insist upon His ethical standards; that His ideal of intellectual greatness is the knowledge of God; that His ideal of emotional function is to love God and our neighbour; that His ideal of volitional fulfilment is to seek first the Kingdom of God.

The Church is not sent to London, or Calcutta, or Pekin, to invite men to consider the claims of a Teacher Whom men may compare with others. She is to announce Him as the crowned Lord, absolute King, the only One Who, having entered into conflict with the forces that unmake humanity, and the enemies that hold humanity enthralled, has crushed and defeated them, coming into the place of final and glorious victory by the way of resurrection. She is to preach the Lordship of Christ to the nations, and thus to bring them under the spell of the announcement. Her responsibility is that of seeing to it that all the nations hear its proclamation. The Church has never been commissioned to convert the world, but to evangelise it, to create its opportunity of choice, to bring men everywhere face to face with the King, that in His presence man may crown or crucify Him; to preach the doctrine of His supremacy, which doctrine becomes to those who hear it a savour of life unto life, or of death unto death, according to whether they obey or rebel. That is the first great and grave responsibility of the Church.

As she fulfils that function, proclaiming the Lordship of Jesus, bringing men under the influence and sway of the love of Christ, compelling them to consider His claim, there will be those who will submit themselves and bend the knee, and yield the heart and life to Him. Such she is commanded to baptize "into the name of the Father and of the Son and of the Holy Ghost." This baptism is in itself a suggestive symbolism. The first thought it conveys is that of death, but baptism is not the victory of death, but a passage through death into life. Thus the rite of baptism suggests death and resurrection. Those who submit to the King are brought into His Kingdom through death and resurrection, not by water baptism, but by the baptism of the Holy Spirit, of which water baptism is a symbol or sign.

Those who come under the influence of the proclamation of the Lordship of Jesus, and yielding to it, pass through His death and resurrection into living union with Him, are to be taught "to observe all things whatsoever I commanded you." They are to realise in their own fellowship the actuality of His Kingship, and are to manifest through their corporate life the glory and grace of the Kingdom of God. This new society is formed wherever, as a result of the proclamation of His Lordship, men and women yield thereto; a society of those who not only believe in His Lordship, but bend to it, and exhibit to the world the result of His Kingship in their individual lives and social fellowship.

If we measure the history of the Christian Church by that great ideal we inevitably see how sorely and grievously she has failed.

Finally, a brief word concerning the dynamic. If the Church is to fulfil this great responsibility, she must enter into the full meaning of the final words of the Lord; "Lo, I am with you all the days, even unto the consummation of the age." We must understand the meaning of the phrase "end of the world." Too often we think of it as some catastrophe or destruction of the earth. That is not the meaning of the words of which the Lord made use. The superior translation is undoubtedly "consummation of the age." The earth will continue long after the completion of this age. The promise is that of the abiding presence of the King through the present age. It is impossible to preach His Lordship prevailingly, save in living fellowship with Himself. We may discuss it and demonstrate it intellectually, but the demonstration will lack compelling power, save as the truth is proclaimed in living, personal comradeship with Him. In His phrase "all the days," is inferred mastery of circumstances, the inference vindicated, as we have seen, by His resurrection. The One Who through defeat proceeded to absolute victory accompanies His people, as in obedience to His command they go forth to proclaim His Kingship.

In the words already dealt with, "the consummation of the age," His ultimate victory is implied. There was no fear of failure in the heart of the King. The age initiated by His first advent will be consummated at His second; and through all the toil He abides with His people, leading them in perpetual triumph as they abide in fellowship with Him.

The realisation of the promise of His abiding presence is entirely dependent upon the Church's willingness to fulfil her responsibility. She has no right to apply this gracious word to herself save as she fulfils the conditions imposed. If we have no passion in our hearts for the discipling of the nations, we have no warrant for believing that He remains in fellowship with us.

THE COMMISSION ACCORDING TO MARK

"Go ye into all the kosmos, and preach the gospel to the whole creation. He that believeth and is baptized shall be saved; but he that disbelieveth shall be condemned."—MARK xvi. 15, 16.

III

THE EVANGEL TO CREATION

THE events chronicled by Mark, and those recorded by Luke and John, occurred on the first day in the resurrection life of Jesus. That was a day full of startling surprises for the disciples. The Cross had been to them the disaster of disasters, blighting their hopes, and scattering them like chaff before the wind. With the dawn of the first day of the week there had come to a little company of waiting, weeping women the consciousness that Jesus was not dead, but alive. A little later He had appeared personally to Mary of Magdala. Peter and John had together looked at the place where He had lain, and had been convinced of supernatural resurrection by the remarkable way in which the grave-cloths still lay undisturbed, as they had been wrapped about His body. At some hour in the day Christ had found Peter, and had a private interview with him. In the same day He had joined two disciples on the way to Emmaus, and to them had opened the Scriptures, finally making Himself known to them in the breaking of the bread. These two, immediately after He had passed out of sight, had hastened back to Jerusalem to tell the ten that they had actually been in company with the risen Lord. Before they could recount what had happened to them, the ten had a story to tell them. They had not seen Jesus, but having heard of the interview with Peter, declared "The Lord is risen indeed, and hath appeared to Simon." Some of them doubted. They were all on the borderland between the light and darkness, and nothing seemed clearly defined or certain.

Suddenly, without the opening of a door, or the shooting of a bolt, or the turning of a key, Jesus stood materially manifest in their midst. Mark, Luke, and John tell the story of that appearing. These stories do not contradict each other. They are quite different in many respects, but they are complementary; and all are needed to a full appreciation of what took place in the upper room on that occasion of His first meeting with the ten. Mark, who in all likelihood received his account from Peter, recorded those words which had supremely impressed Peter. Luke, the artist historian, gathering up the testimony of eye-witnesses and putting them in order for his friend Theophilus, recorded the words which he accounted of supreme importance. John recorded words, the deepest and profoundest, omitted by the others in all probability because the mystic note was beyond their comprehension.

The Gospel according to Mark is that which pre-eminently reveals Jesus as the Servant of God. It is interesting to remember that the book of the Old Testament which reveals the Servant of God is the prophecy of Isaiah. To that prophecy Mark made reference in the very first sentences of his Gospel, when introducing the herald of Messiah he declared that he came in fulfilment of the prophecy of Isaiah, which foretold the sending of a messenger to prepare the way of the Lord.

In the messages of the ancient prophet there are evidences of his almost overwhelming sense of the polluting effect upon the whole earth of the sin of man. Perhaps this is most pointedly and clearly declared in the twenty-fourth chapter. When we turn to the Gospel of Mark we find that he chronicled the words in the commission of Jesus which reveal the fact that the ultimate purpose of His mission was that of the redemption and renewal of the whole creation through the salvation of individual men.

In our consideration of this aspect of the commission we shall again seek to discover the deposit, the debt, and the dynamic.

First, then, as to the deposit, that particular truth committed to the Church, for the proclamation of which she is held responsible. This is only suggested by one inclusive word, which, standing alone, is characterised by indefiniteness. The word "gospel" is inclusive, but it needs explanation if we would understand the nature of the deposit suggested.

The inclusive context illuminates the indefinite word, until it becomes perfectly clear. We must however, take time to consider that context patiently, in order to understand what our Lord meant by the term "the gospel" on this occasion. Now if we can read this story with the same naturalness that would characterise our reading of it for the first time, we shall be greatly helped. This is not easy to do, the reason being that we have constantly recited the commission in separation from its context. Indeed, it may safely be affirmed that very few without careful examination are at all conscious of the fact that while the commission is a separate and distinct command it nevertheless here constitutes one link in a continuous story; and it is perfectly certain that it can only be accurately interpreted as that is remembered. To treat the commission without reference to the context makes it necessary to attempt to formulate an exposition of what Jesus meant by the term "the gospel." To consider the commission as a part of a continuous story is to discover the fact that He meant one thing.

Let us first then, examine that story in order to discover the sequence of events. We need go no further back than the ninth verse. Beginning there we discover the sequence.

Jesus appeared to Mary of Magdala. She carried the news to the mourning disciples that she had actually seen Him alive, and they *disbelieved.*

He appeared in another form to two on the way to Emmaus. These also returned and told the story, and still they *did not believe.*

Finally, He stood in the upper room, and His first words were those in which He rebuked this unbelief, and then immediately said, "Go ye . . . and preach the gospel . . . he that believeth . . . shall be saved . . . he that disbelieveth shall be condemned."

In order that we may be perfectly clear

about this, let us mark the sequence in other words. Mary of Magdala declared she had seen the living Lord. The disciples did not believe this. Two men who walked to Emmaus declared that they had seen the living Lord. The disciples did not believe it. Jesus upbraided them for this unbelief, and then said, "Go . . . and preach the gospel . . . he that believeth . . . shall be saved . . . he that disbelieveth shall be condemned."

What then is "the gospel"? It is the good news that the Lord is risen. It may be affirmed that this is a narrowing of the intention of the great word in this commission; that nothing is said of the teaching of Jesus, the life of Jesus, the Cross of Jesus. As a matter of fact all these are involved in resurrection, and become parts of the gospel because of the resurrection. If we only have the teaching of Jesus, we have no gospel. If we only have the account of His perfect life, we have no gospel. If we only have the Cross, we have no gospel. All these become part of the gospel because of its central truth, which is that of the resurrection. The deposit then, the essential and central truth referred to in this phase of the commission, is that of the actual resurrection of Jesus from among the dead. The resurrection of Jesus was the demonstration of His perfect victory over all opposing forces; and of the fact that His victory enabled Him to baptize such as believe in Him into union with His life.

In demonstration of the truth of the latter part of this assertion, let His words immediately following be carefully considered. "He that believeth and is baptized shall be saved; but he that disbelieveth shall be condemned. And these signs shall follow them that believe, in My Name shall they cast out demons; they shall speak with new tongues; they shall take up serpents, and if they drink any deadly thing, it shall in no wise hurt them; they shall lay hands on the sick, and they shall recover." It is of the utmost importance that we carefully observe that the Lord did not say that these signs should accompany the preacher. The idea is not that those who proclaim the resurrection shall work these signs as evidences of the truth of resurrection. The actual statement is that "these signs shall follow them that believe." All men believing on Him were, as the result of His resurrection, to be brought into possession of that life whose forces operate in the ways suggested. By this I do not say that the preachers were not able to do the things described, but that the signs were not peculiar gifts bestowed upon men, equipping them for work. They were rather evidences of the new ability granted to such as believe the evangel.

Let us mark the suggestiveness of all this when taken, as it must be taken, in connection with the term "the gospel." "The gospel" is that of the risen Lord. His resurrection means that He has mastered death, and therefore has overcome all the destructive forces operating in creation—such forces as have spoiled and blighted humanity, and through the spoiling of humanity have blighted and spoiled the whole creation. Whether these forces be supernatural, those who believe in His

Name shall be able to cast them out. Whether they be the forces of social disorder, which began with Babel and its confusion of tongues, those who believe shall have the new articulation, "they shall speak with new tongues," and thus come to new mutual understanding. Whether they be the forces that are destructive in the material realm; serpents, or poison, or sickness; serpents and poison, the symbols of the destructive forces of nomadic or savage peoples; or sickness, the destructive force resulting from civilisation; those who believe enter into the realm of mastery over the former, and receive healing for all the latter.

The risen Lord is Himself the Master of all destructive forces, and those who, coming into living union with Him through His resurrection receive of His strength, are also to gain victories over these forces.

What then, is the picture that rises before the mind as one reads this commission in its necessary relation to the context? It is that of the risen Lord as the Renewer of creation, as the One Who, passing through death into the place of resurrection victory, becomes not merely the Saviour of the spirits of men, but the Renewer of the whole territory of human life; and therefore the One Whose power will be felt in all the creation that lies beneath man which has been polluted and spoiled by his touch. In the twenty-fourth chapter of Isaiah, to which we have already made reference, these words occur, "The earth also is polluted under the inhabitants thereof; because they have transgressed the laws, changed the ordinance, broken the everlasting covenant." Let us place by the side of that word of Isaiah the word of Paul, "The whole creation groaneth and travaileth in pain together until now."

If the first phase of the Missionary Manifesto was that of the absolute Lordship of Jesus, which the Church is to affirm and declare, the second is that of the risen Jesus Who is Renewer and Restorer of the whole creation.

This is the great glad news committed to the Church, and we have been in danger of minimising the meaning of the gospel. Our outlook has been appallingly narrow;

and we have disastrously failed to see the application of the fact of the resurrection of Christ to the whole creation. Our failure to discover His meaning does not mean His failure to work His purposes out to final fulfilment. He is the risen Lord, and is therefore Master of death. He is also therefore, Master of all the forces that spoil, and is able to renew everything that has been corrupted.

What then, in this respect is our debt? At this point the commission leaves us in no doubt. The words of Jesus are perfectly clear. "Go ye into all the kosmos, and herald the evangel to the whole creation." A natural reading of these words should immediately arrest attention by reason of the inclusive nature of the terms, "the kosmos," and "the whole creation."

By translating the former "the world" we have been at least in danger of thinking that our Lord's reference was to humanity only. As a matter of fact it is a far more comprehensive term, which He interprets by the second of the phrases referred to, "the whole creation." To take the first term, "the kosmos," and to trace the history of the word, is to be admitted to the larger outlook. The Greek word kosmos originally signified an ornament, or something beautiful. It was a word used entirely in the realm of art. In process of time, long before the ministry of Jesus was exercised or these gospel stories were written, the word acquired a more spacious meaning, and was used in reference to the whole universe, because the Greek mind came to an understanding of the fact that the universe is beautiful and orderly. Then again, as the Greek mind failed to grasp the truth of the spiritual, the word passed back into a more restricted use, and was applied to the material frame in the midst of which man lives his life. In the days in which John made use of it—and it was peculiarly his word among New Testament writers—it referred to the earth and the heavens enwrapping it, the heaven of the atmosphere and the heaven of the stellar spaces, that system of which our planet is so small a part.

It will thus be seen that the word stands

for much more than the people who lived upon the surface of the earth. It refers to the whole earth in its order, its beauty, and its forces. The declaration of the Old Testament—

> "The earth is Jehovah's, and the fulness thereof;
> The world, and they that dwell therein,"

suggests all that is included in the term "kosmos."

Jesus made use of the word in this simple sense as including the earth and the fulness thereof, all its hidden treasures, its boundless resources, and its yet undiscovered secrets. He recognised that the whole earth in all its fulness needed His evangel, not merely men and women, but beasts and birds and flowers, in order to the discovery and utilisation of the secret resources of the earth. So that the whole may become a thing of glorious beauty, the earth needs the redemption of the King.

That we may have added light on this subject let us turn to other passages of Scripture. In the Book of Genesis we have a wonderful picture of creation rising by the will of God, and by His power, scale upon scale, ever higher, until at last by a new and distinct act of God, He, taking the highest thing in the lower creation, by inbreathing separated it by infinite distances from everything that lies beneath it. He created man, and by the last act in the creative process made him infinitely more than an animal. Having thus created him, He gave him dominion over all the creation beneath him to which he was linked by the earlier processes of his making. That creation was placed under his control in order to its development and perfecting. Man in the image and likeness of God, was placed where he might act in fellowship with God for the discovery of the hidden secrets of the earth, and the bringing of them to ultimate perfection.

Turning to the Book of Psalms, that wonderful literature of Hebrew expectation and hope and confidence, we hear one of the singers of Israel as he first inquires—

"What is man, that Thou art mindful of him?"

and then, as in harmony with the original story of creation, he declares—

"Thou hast put all things under his feet:
All sheep and oxen,
Yea, and the beasts of the field;
The fowl of the air, and the fish of the sea,
Whatsoever passeth through the paths of the seas."

We pass to the New Testament, and the writer of the letter to the Hebrews, a logician as well as a poet, declares, after quoting from the singer of Israel, that all the Divine intention is seen realised in Christ as representative Man. "Now we see not yet all things subjected to Him. But we behold Him Who hath been made a little lower than the angels, even Jesus." He thus affirmed that while all things are not yet seen under the perfect dominion of man, Jesus is seen, the risen Christ, and the vision of Him is the assurance that the whole creation will yet be redeemed from its groaning and travailing in pain, and realise the fulness of its beauty and glory.

If that threefold picture, or rather that one picture presented in the three parts of our Bible be clearly seen, then the meaning of this commission will be correctly understood. Man in the economy of God is king of the kosmos, but he has lost his sceptre, has lost the key of the mysteries of the world in which he lives, and cannot govern it as he ought to govern, is unable to realise the creation that lies beneath him. Therefore the kingdom of man is a devastated kingdom, because he is a discrowned king; or in the language of Isaiah, "the earth also is polluted under the inhabitants therof." Man's moral disease has permeated the material universe; or as Paul said, "the whole creation groaneth and travaileth in pain together until now . . . waiting for the manifestation of the sons of God." Man's moral regeneration will permeate the material universe, and issue in its remaking,

In the upper room on the day of His resurrection, Jesus stood in the midst of a group of disciples who were so filled with fear that they had gathered within barred doors. He stood there as the Man of God in the midst of creation, Who had regained the sceptre, and had mastered death and all the forces destructive of the creation. He was there as Redeemer, Regenerator, Renewer, "the Firstborn from among the dead," communicating His victorious life to others, and through them to the whole creation.

To this group of men He spoke words of reproof for their unbelief, and commanded them that they should go into the kosmos and herald the gospel of His resurrection to the whole creation. Thus He gave to these men, the first representatives of the Church, as He also gives to the Church to-day, the charge to pass out into contact with the kosmos, and to proclaim to the whole creation the triumphant story of His victory.

Our responsibility to Him is that we obey. Our debt to the world is that we obey. Chaos created the agony of the Cross. Wherever He came into the midst of disorder, He suffered. He, before Whose vision there flamed perpetually the glory of the Divine ideal, felt the anguish of God in the presence of the degradation of that ideal.

All wounds and weariness, all sin and sorrow, not only of man, but through man in creation, surged upon His heart in waves of anguish. He called His disciples into fellowship with Himself in this suffering. That for evermore settles the question of the monastic ideal, as it reveals how completely it is opposed to the method of Jesus. The suffering of the flowers can never be cured if we do not touch them. The agony of the birds can never be ended save as we care for them. The earth can never be lifted from its dulness and deadness, and made to blossom into glorious harvest, save as it is touched by the life of renewed humanity. That is the story of the sufferings of Christ. He came into the world, Himself of the eternal Order, full of grace and truth, and in the consciousness of chaos and disorder He suffered. To press that far enough, and to consider it long enough, is to come to the profound and ultimate note in the mystery of atonement. If we indeed have crowned Him, and His life is in us, we shall be "partakers of His sufferings."

Such suffering results in healing, as it makes possible the communication of the virtue of the strong life to the weak, in order to its strengthening. In our former consideration we referred to the words of Jesus, "be not afraid of them which kill the body, but are not able to kill the soul." That great injunction has many possibilities of application. Let us reverently remember that Jesus Himself is the supreme exposition of it; and moreover, that its ultimate value is discovered in this application. He gave His body to bruising and buffeting and death, having no fear of such as killed the body; but by doing so He liberated the forces of His life that by their liberation they might become the renewing, regenerating forces of men, and through men of the whole creation. The Cross will never have won its final victory until the new heavens and the new earth are established as the result of His redeeming and regenerating work. That is the goal towards which we are to look in all our service.

Therefore the perpetual principle of missionary endeavour is that of passing into the kosmos, and so into the suffering, and thus into ability to communicate renewing forces. The principle is supremely illustrated occasionally, but is constantly manifest in the Christian life. The supreme illustrations are contained in the story of those who, like their Lord and Master, have laid down their lives. Through them the spiritual forces have been liberated, and the results in the world have been far greater than can be measured. It is by virtue communicated, the actual expenditure of force through suffering that the gospel is preached to the whole creation.

All this work must be done in the right order. The Church must ever commence by the proclamation of the evangel to men. To go to the material world, either in garden or city, and to attempt to reconstruct it in order that it may remake men is to invert the Divine order, and to fail. The Church must always begin with man, but she must not forget that the emphasis of this commission is that the ultimate result of man's remaking is that of the renewal of the whole reation. The kosmos will be redeemed when man, who is king of the kosmos, is regenerate. He will be able to restore it to its order, and lead it to the fulfilment of Divine purpose.

Many practical illustrations of this might be given. Take one of the simplest. The garden of a truly Christian man ought to be the most beautiful in the whole district. When it is not so, it is because he is not living in the full power of the risen Christ. When the garden of the ungodly man flourishes it is always because he is availing himself of discoveries that have come as the result of the co-operation of renewed men with God. I sometimes think that if I am to judge the Christianity of London by looking at its gardens, it is an extremely poor thing. Let us keep hold of the philosophy of the simple illustration. That conception of Christian responsibility which aims at the saving of individual men, while it is utterly careless of the groaning of creation, is entirely out of harmony with the meaning of this commission. The home of the Christian man ought to be a microcosm of the Millennial Kingdom; and all the things of God's dear world—and how He loves it, flowers, and birds, and forces—ought to feel the touch of redeemed humanity, and be lifted into fuller life thereby.

We pass finally to the subject of the dynamic. This is no more clearly revealed than is the deposit, but it is as certainly involved. When Jesus said, "He that believeth and is baptized, shall be saved; but he that disbelieveth shall be condemned," He suggested a response on the part of God to a certain attitude on the part of man. The alternative attitudes are described in the phrases, "he that believeth," "he that disbelieveth." The ultimate results are described in the words "shall be saved" and "shall be condemned." The dynamic phrase is "and is baptized." That refers to the work of God. No man can baptize himself, or be baptized by another. Essential baptism is baptism in the Spirit. Water baptism is symbolic. In the moment in which a man believes, he is baptized by God in the Spirit, and so into the resurrection life of Jesus, and therefore he is saved. If a man disbelieve, he is not saved, but rather condemned because he does not enter into the regenerate life, seeing that he lacks baptism in the Spirit. The suggestion of these words is that as we herald the evangel of the Cross we do so in co-operation with the risen Lord, so that when men hearing the evangel, believe, they are immediately baptized into living union with the living Christ, and so come into possession of the regenerative forces which being applied, produce the restoration of creation.

The revelation of these words then, is that those who fulfil this commission shall be accompanied by the Lord Himself, co-operating with them in the communication of life by the Spirit, to those who believe their message. Men who hear and believe shall receive this power. The man who believes shall gain victory over spiritual forces, he shall cast out devils; over all social disorder, he shall speak with new tongues; over all destructive forces, poisons, and serpents, and sicknesses. The man who hearing, disbelieves, will remain in the grip of devils, in the confusion of Babel, the prey of the destructive forces which work in

Nature. The mastery of the forces in Nature that spoil is possible through regenerative men. We must not neglect any force which God has put in the universe, nor count the healing virtues of trees and plants as outside His economy. In the power of His resurrection life man discovers and uses the whole creation by mastery over it, in order that it may minister to him, according to God's first intention.

In order to fulfilment of such responsibility the first necessity is that of a living experience of the risen Lord. There is no healing virtue in the doctrine of resurrection. The healing virtue flows through the risen Lord. No healing virtue can be communicated by orthodox announcement of the fact of His resurrection. The healing virtue can only be communicated by those through whom the life of the risen Lord is flowing.

Not only must there be this living experience of the risen Lord, there must be obedience to His command. We must go into the kosmos, placing our lives in contact with creation, and pouring them out therein, in order that by such sacrifice creation may be renewed.

If the first note of the Missionary Manifesto be the proclamation of the Lordship of Christ, the second note is the proclamation of the risen Lord as the Renewer of the whole creation; and the only way in which that proclamation can be made is by passing into the kosmos in order to communicate to it through sacrificial service the forces of our own Christ-renewed life. We have done nothing to heal the groaning of creation when we have discovered the glory of the gospel. We have done nothing toward the final victory until in fellowship with our Lord we have put the actual forces of our life so at the disposal of the debased and the degraded as to know the experience of suffering, and that weakening by the way, which is of the nature of death. It is when the Church begins to see the suffering of creation with eyes washed by tears, and when she puts herself into such close relation with the wounded world as to share its agony, and as to release her own life blood to heal it, that this commission will be obeyed.

THE COMMISSION ACCORDING TO LUKE

"Ye are witnesses of these things. And behold, I send forth the promise of My Father upon you: but tarry ye in the city, until ye be clothed with power from on high."—LUKE xxiv. 48–49.

IV

THE WITNESSES

THE third Gospel was written by a Greek to a Greek. Luke, the beloved physician, a man of culture, with the genius of the artist, wrote for his friend Theophilus a treatise "concerning all that Jesus began both to do and to teach." Greece in the brief and brilliant days of its greatness, gave to the world for so small a country, and so brief a history, more men of outstanding personal greatness than any other people has produced. She never came to anything like national influence of a lasting nature. While Greek influence has permeated history, and obtains to-day, it was created by the strength of her individual sons, rather than by her realisation of the inter-relationships between men as they result in a Commonwealth. The dominant factor in Greek greatness and influence was that of her passion for the perfection of the individual.

The writer of this Gospel was under the influence of that passion, and he found in Jesus the One Who both filled and destroyed the Greek ideal. With inimitable skill Luke, in the earlier parts of his treatise, portrayed the perfection of his Master. This portrayal proceeds along the natural line of development, as it presents first the *physical* in the story of the birth; and then proceeds to record what no other evangelist refers to, the *mental* development as manifest in what to-day we should describe as the period of adolescence; finally telling of how, in the fulness of manhood, the essential *spiritual* life came to its perfection for service by the mystic anointing of the Holy Spirit.

Beyond that, he shows how that perfect Personality was vocationally perfected through processes of temptation, and teaching, until it reached the crowning glory of the transfiguration mount. The vision of

Jesus on the mount of transfiguration is that of the fulfilment of the highest and richest conceptions of Greek idealism.

The story however, is not finished. Luke has now to tell how, to the amazement of lovers and friends, He turned His back upon that mountain height, and passing through the valley of suffering, set His face towards the cross which, as Paul the friend of Luke declared, was to the Greek foolishness. To the Greek it must indeed have been unutterable foolishness, for the Cross spoiled the individual perfection, and broke as into a thousand fragments the great ideal. As imaginatively I watch Luke at his work, I seem to see him with growing wonder setting forth the developing perfection of this Man, until all the highest and best of that system of philosophy in which he had been trained was fulfilled before his eyes in the radiant splendour of the crowned humanity on the holy mount. Then I seem to see him amazed and perplexed as he follows the history until he sees the beauty marred by the disfigurement of the brutal Cross.

If that had been all the story, perhaps Luke had never written it, for so far it is the story of an unutterable disaster. The supreme and overwhelming marvel was that of the resurrection, wherein this Man returned, out of the mystery of shameful death, in a glory more radiant than that in which He had stood upon the mountain height; the very wounds of His disfigurement having become the supreme unveilings of the hitherto unrevealed glory. The mould of Greek idealism was shattered into a thousand fragments by the perfection of Jesus. It could not contain Him. Beyond the foolishness of the Cross, He stood arrayed in garments of light and glory, Himself effulgent with a beauty which had never entered into the conception of Greek philosophy. Luke saw this Man bringing out of death a mystic power, enabling Him to communicate the dynamic of His own human perfection to the bruised and battered sons of men. Those whom Greek idealism would treat with contempt by reason of their failure, were healed and remade, and themselves came into conformity to the likeness of His glory.

The resurrection stories as told by Luke emphasise the identity of the Person Whom the disciples met after the Cross with Him Whom they had known before it; and indicate the fact that He had entered into another life, in which all the limitations of the days of His flesh had passed away for ever.

He tells of how He walked to Emmaus, unknown by men who had been familiar with Him; and then of how He revealed Himself to them in the breaking of the bread, so that no doubt remained that it was indeed their own Lord and Master.

When they were gathered in the upper room, and all the doors were locked, He presenced Himself amongst them, without the opening of a door, and so amazed them that they could not believe for very joy and wonder. Then in order to allay their fears, and demonstrate His identity, He showed them His hands and His feet, and asking for food, partook of the broiled fish which they provided.

When Luke writes for his friend Theophilus the words of the final commission, he records those which, in harmony with his Gospel, emphasise the fact that the responsibility of the Church is that of revealing to the world the perfections of Jesus as fulfilling in Himself the highest ideals of individual life, and as accomplishing through the mystery of His Cross that which makes possible the remaking of those who have failed. "Ye are witnesses of these things."

So that, as in the gospel of the Kingship, the commission charges us to proclaim the royalty of Jesus; and in the gospel of the perfect Servant, the commission charges us to share in His suffering and saving service; in the gospel of the perfections of the Son of God, the commission charges us that we are to reveal these perfections to the world as witnesses, representing by reproduction. Here, so far as our responsibility is concerned, we reach the most stupendous note in the missionary commission. We shall follow the same lines of consideration as those adopted in the previous studies—those namely, of the deposit of truth, the debt of responsibility, and the dynamic of accomplishment.

These divisions are perfectly patent, and may thus be summarised. The deposit is indicated in the phrase "these things"; the debt is revealed in the declaration, "ye are witnesses"; and the dynamic is indicated in the promise and the charge, "I send forth the promise of My Father upon you; but tarry ye in the city, until ye be clothed with power from on high."

First then, as to the deposit. "These things." What things? The answer to that inquiry must be discovered in the context. The text in itself is incomplete, and to consider it alone might be to misinterpret the meaning of the Master. It is well therefore, that we should read again the words of Jesus immediately preceding:—

"These are My words which I spake unto you, while I was yet with you, how that all things must needs be fulfilled, which are written in the law of Moses, and the prophets, and the Psalms, concerning Me."

"Thus it is written, that the Christ should suffer, and rise again from the dead the third day."

"And that repentance and remission of sins should be preached in His name unto all the nations, beginning from Jerusalem."

"Ye are witnesses of these things."

It is evident that the meaning of the Master's phrase, "these things," must be discovered by a consideration of these words. The things referred to fall into three divisions. In the first He claimed that in His ministry there was fulfilment of the economy of the past; "All things must needs be fulfilled which are written in the law of Moses, and the prophets, and the Psalms." He claimed in the second place that the way of fulfilment was that of His own suffering and resurrection; "Thus it is written, that the Christ should suffer, and rise again from the dead the third day." He claimed finally that the issue of His suffering and resurrection was the initiation of a new method of moral and spiritual reconstruction for men; "That repentance and remission of sins should be preached in His name."

Of "these things"—the fulfilment of the ancient economy; the suffering and glory of

Christ; the reconstruction of human nature —we are to be witnesses.

First as to the fulfilment of the past. The Hebrew dispensation had been one of hope and of expectation, of type and shadow and suggestion; and its three outstanding qualities are indicated by the threefold content of the Old Testament Scriptures, to which our Lord referred in the language perfectly familiar to the men of His day, as "the law, the prophets, and the Psalms."

In the law of Moses was contained the revelation of the will of God for man. It may be spoken of as the presentation of the ideal.

The history of the people was that of failure to realise the ideal, and in that section of the Scriptures described as "the prophets" which contained in the Hebrew Bible not only the books which we describe as prophetic but the books of history, we have the teaching which corrects the failure and recalls to the original ideal.

In the Psalms, which contain the songs of men in all conditions and under all circumstances, and reveal their aspirations, we have the prayers of desire, the longings of the human heart after the realisation of that ideal presented in the law, and defended in the prophets.

The initial economy therefore, had been that of the presentation of the ideal, the ministry of correction, and the experience of hope.

The claim of Christ was that all these things were fulfilled in Him; that He had fulfilled the ideal; that in life and teaching He had vindicated the prophetic utterances; that in His ministry He fulfilled all the hopes and aspirations of the past. As the law had been the expression of the master-principle of individual and social life, that namely of the government of God, He fulfilled the ideal in personal experience and in authoritative exposition. The corrections of the Divine patience, in the march of history, in the thunder of the prophet against sin, and in his sorrow over failure, were all repeated and finally stated in His own ministry, insisting as it did upon the holiness of God and the compassion of His heart. The aspirations of the human heart as revealed in that most wonderful collection of devotional utterances, wherein, under the guidance of the Spirit of God, humanity sang out all its emotion, were all answered in Him, and through Him, in the experience of such as were brought into living association with Him.

The stupendous and magnificent claim of Christ was that all these things of the past found fulfilment in Him; and the charge He laid upon His disciples was that they were to be witnesses of these things.

By this commission then, we are sent into the world in order that by what we are the world may know that the highest ideals are fulfilled in Christ, and in those in whom the Christ life dwells; that the corrections of all prophetic utterance may be obeyed through the Christ; that the aspirations of the past find their answer in such as share His life.

We pass reverently to the second phase of responsibility, that namely of being witnesses to the fact of the suffering and glory of Christ. In that is contained the whole story of the mission of Christ, that mission whereby He does not only fulfil the past, but initiates the new. The thought of fulfilment necessarily involves that of transition. From the old which presented ideals, corrected failures, and inspired hope, we come presently to the new, that which bestows repentance and remission of sins, so that there may be realisation. Between these lay the actual work of the Christ, His suffering and His glory, His travail and His triumph, His death and His resurrection. He is seen standing between the two, fulfilling the expectation of the old, creating the energy for the new, and He does so by the way of death and resurrection. Through His witnesses these things are to be unfolded to the world. Through them the world is to see the suffering Christ. Through them the world is to see the risen Christ.

At this point it is of supreme importance that we remind ourselves of that to be considered more fully later, that witnessing is infinitely more than preaching. The doctrine of the Cross becomes dynamic in crucified lives. The truth of the resurrection becomes triumphant through lives transfigured by resurrection.

The final phase of witness is that of the result produced by the death and resurrection of Christ. Moral reconstruction is both demonstration of the resurrection and exposition of the Cross. The process of moral reconstruction is here indicated in the suggestive words, "repentance and remission of sins," repentance being the human attitude, and remission of sins the Divine answer. Moral reconstruction always begins in human repentance, but it is never completed save in Divine remission of sins. Repentance is the desire in man for renewal and reconstruction. Apart from it no man is ever regenerated or renewed. Remission of sins is the answer of God to that repentance. Where there is no repentance there can be no remission. Genuine repentance based on faith, and expressing itself in faith, is always answered by remission of sins. The importance of the inter-relation between these cannot be over-stated. The only hope of moral reconstruction is that of repentance.

The wonder of the work of Christ is

that He gives that repentance, and the responsibility of the Church is that it witnesses to that fact. To stand in the presence of the awful purity of Christ is to come into the place of repentance. For the moment we are not discussing the ultimate issue. It is true that a man may repent, and yet go back upon his repentance. But repentance itself is in this sense the gift of Christ. It comes by the way of His illumination. It is generated by the flashing of the light of His life upon the life of a man. It is the changed mind in regard to God, and with regard to sin. The Church's responsibility is that of bearing such witness to the purity of Christ, and the glory of that purity, as to produce such a repentance in the lives of sinning men. Wherever that repentance is yielded to, there immediately follows the remission of sins. That is infinitely more than forgiveness. It is that of the loosing of the soul from sin, the breaking of the chain, the quenching of the fire, the negation of the poison. It is the act of God. He is able to remit sins, because of the death and resurrection of

Christ. These are the foundations upon which, and upon which alone, He remits sins. The Church's responsibility is that of witnessing to the fact of remission by lives in which sin has lost its power.

We are therefore witnesses to the world of the fact of the fulfilment of the initial economy in Christ; of the way by which He fulfilled that economy through His own death and resurrection; and of the results issuing from such fulfilment, repentance in man, and remission of sins as the act of God.

An experimental illustration of that contextual interpretation is found in one of the most fascinating pictures in the book of the Acts of the Apostles. Peter and the apostles had been arrested, and stood before the Sadducean high priest, and those associated with him; charged with having filled Jerusalem with their teaching, and with intending to bring the blood of Jesus upon these men. Peter replied in words characterised by directness and finality, "We must obey God rather than men." Then in a few sentences he stated the whole burden of the apostolic message, "The God of our fathers raised up Jesus, Whom ye slew, hanging Him on a tree. Him did God exalt with His right hand to be a Prince and a Saviour, for to give repentance to Israel, and remission of sins."

This statement was immediately followed by the significant claim, "And we are witnesses of these things." The relation of the commission to this incident of obedience is patent. Jesus had said, "Ye are witnesses of these things." Peter affirmed, "We are witnesses of these things." According to Jesus "these things" were those of His fulfilment of the initial economy, of His death and resurrection, of His ability to bestow repentance and remission of sins upon man. According to Peter "these things" included the recognition of the relation of the mission of Jesus to the ancient economy, for he spoke of "the God of our fathers"; of the death and resurrection of Jesus, for he declared "God raised up Jesus, Whom ye slew"; of the result of the exaltation of Jesus, for he affirmed "Him did God exalt with His right hand to be a Prince and a Saviour, for to give repentance to Israel, and remission of sins."

What then, is the debt resulting from the possession of the deposit? The inquiry is answered as we understand the meaning of the word "witnesses." The term suggests three ideas, which may be indicated by the words "realisation," "manifestation," and "proclamation." A witness is one who has realised the ideals of Jesus by appropriation of His grace. He is one therefore, through whom the perfection of the ideals and the power of grace are manifested to the world. He is moreover, one who is called upon to proclaim to men that evangel which discovers to them the secret of how he has realised that which he manifests. This is the thought of witnessing as interpreted by all the writings of the New Testament.

In order to witness bearing there must first be realisation. It is necessary moreover, that we understand that realisation means making real in experience, which is infinitely more than apprehending intellectually. No man or woman or child can witness for Christ who has not realised "these things" in personal experience. In a previous study we summarised the ideals of Jesus as those of the supremacy of the spiritual, and the inwardness of morality. To witness for Christ then, is to live the life which at all times and under all circumstances recognises the supremacy of the spiritual; which constantly recognises that the material is none other than the carbon upon which the essential light of the spiritual is revealed. A witness also is one who makes no boast in the accidentals of an external morality, but who is pure in heart. He is moreover, one to whom there has come the vision of the glory of the ultimate establishment of the Kingdom of God, and for whom the realisation of that vision becomes the master-passion and purpose of life.

Or we may state this truth concerning the realisation in the terms of the contextual interpretation, which we have considered. A witness is one in whom the ideals of the past are fulfilled by the power of Christ; one in whom the Cross and the resurrection accomplish their respective missions; one who experiences the abiding consciousness of repentance, with the constant triumph of the remission of sins.

Wherever this realisation is found, manifestation ensues. The whole fact may be briefly stated by the declaration that witnesses are those who at all times, and in all places, and under all circumstances, reveal Christ. It is impossible to make this statement without a consciousness of shame filling the spirit. Here we have so grievously failed. Let us speak therefore, only in the language which is possible to us, as we affirm that the measure in which we are witnesses for Christ is the measure in which we manifest Him, as the result of experimental realisation. If manifestation fail, it is because realisation has failed.

Following realisation and manifestation, there must be proclamation. The witnesses must tell the secret of how their own lives have been transformed. There is certainly need for a new emphasis of this last phase of responsibility. It is perfectly true that proclamation apart from manifestation is of no value, and that the testimony of life is the most powerful in fulfilment of responsibility. It is equally true however, that so surely as there is manifestation there will be inquiry. Seeing the glory of Christ, and the revelation of His power in the lives of men, others will desire to know the secrets of realisation. The witness must be ready to answer all such inquiry. The symbol of the Church's service is the tongue of fire. The tongue apart from the fire is useless, but the fire demands the tongue in order that it may give expression to the laws which govern its purifying and energising force. If in the lives of His people Christ is victorious, and through them is manifest, then they must be ready to speak to those in their own home, to those they meet in social life, to those with whom they come in contact in all the ways of life, of Him Who has given them repentance and remission of sins, declaring that their deliverance has come by His Cross, and their realisation by His resurrection. For this testimony the world is waiting, and the Church is responsible to her Lord, and in debt to the whole race to realise, to manifest, to proclaim "these things."

Such a responsibility must produce a sense of almost overwhelming shame in the presence of past failure, and of equally overwhelming fear in the consciousness of present inability. If there were no word in this phase of the commission clearly indicating the power in which it is possible to obey, we hardly dare venture upon the pathway of obedience. The first two phases of the commission with which we have dealt seem to be much easier to obey than this. To proclaim His royalty; even to go into the presence of all the suffering of creation in order to announce His evangel; these things may indeed be conceived of, and we might even venture to attempt them. But when we hear this declaration, which makes it patent that neither the one nor the other can be done save as in our own lives, we realise, and through them manifest the Christ Himself, we are brought face to face with the supreme consciousness of our need of "power from on high"; and that is exactly what He promises. Let us hear His actual words, "Behold, I send forth the promise of My Father upon you: but tarry ye in the city, until ye be clothed with power from on high." Thus as He reveals the deposit, and declares the debt, He promises the dynamic. It is only in the power of the fulness of the Holy Spirit that it is possible to realise the deposit or discharge the debt. In that power both are possible. To be possessed by the Spirit is to have found the secret of realisation, and consequently to possess the power of manifestation. We shall never realise the things of Christ by contemplation or by imitation. These can only be realised as we share His life, and that life can only be shared by the indwelling of the Holy Spirit.

It is through such realisation by the indwelling Spirit that manifestation becomes possible. Every victory which the Spirit wins for Christ in the believer, is a victory won for Christ through the believer.

It is equally true that the secret of persuasive proclamation is neither human eloquence nor human argument. To refer again to the experimental illustration of the Acts of the Apostles, Peter not only said, "we are witnesses of these things," he added, "and so also is the Holy Ghost, Whom God hath given to them that obey Him." In the power of that Spirit we realise, we manifest, we proclaim, the Christ.

The final word therefore, was necessarily that which the Lord uttered, "Tarry ye . . . until ye be clothed with power from on high." The principle of that injunction has abiding application, but the application is changed. The abiding principle is the recognition of the fact that witnessing is impossible, save in the power of the Holy Spirit. Human judgment and human energy are alike insufficient. We may plan our work, and even work our plan, and yet no victories be won. We may arrange our boards and our committees, and conduct our campaigns, and yet not discharge our debt. Until the breath of God pass over the valley, all these things are but dry bones. For all missionary endeavour, whether in the home-land or in the distant places of the world, the supreme necessity is that of the power of the Spirit, and save as that power is bestowed it is infinitely better than nothing should be attempted.

But if the principle abides, the application is changed. The tarrying of the apostles was necessary. For fifty days between the resurrection and Pentecost they waited. For the last ten days they waited in absolute inability to witness. Their Lord had ascended, and the Spirit had not yet been given. There was no blame attached to them for tarrying. The only mistake they made, if indeed they made any, was that they attempted to fill the vacancy in their own number, before the coming of the Spirit.

Their tarrying was necessary, but our tarrying is unnecessary, because the power is immediately available. "Tarry . . . until ye be clothed with power from on high." Do not touch the work of God save in the fulness of the Spirit. But why do we lack the fulness of the Spirit? After ten days of waiting the day of Pentecost came, and with it the Holy Spirit. That Spirit has never been withdrawn, and so far as we may refer to His presence in the terms of time or space, we affirm that any building in which the saints of God assemble to-day is as full of the Holy Spirit as was the upper room on the day of Pentecost.

If we are not filled with the Spirit, the blame is on us. If there be malice in the heart, rebellion in the life, impurity in the thinking; if there be wilful persistence in disobedience, then let us tarry, let us resign all our offices, and in the interests of the Kingdom of God, stand outside the Church's fellowship.

But let us clearly understand that we must not compare our tarryings with that of the apostles, and by so doing put the blame of our incompetence upon God. We live in the age of the Spirit. The laws of His operation are fully known, and the "power from on high" is immediately at the disposal of all such as are obedient to those laws. To wait for the sound of a rushing, mighty wind, for the sight of visible tongues of fire, for ability in ecstatic mood to utter speech that needs interpretation, is to forget that these are not the only, or the final, or the highest signs of the presence and power of the Spirit. Indeed, these were the simpler signs of a dawning age, and they passed as men came to fuller realisation of the full meaning of the spiritual equipment.

Our responsibility therefore, in this particular is that we make no attempt to witness save in the power of the Spirit; and that we immediately, and at whatever cost, cease to resist, or grieve, or quench the Spirit; and by absolute abandonment of ourselves to the Lord, avail ourselves of the power placed at the disposal of the Church on the day of Pentecost, and never withdrawn.

THE COMMISSION ACCORDING TO JOHN

"As the Father hath sent Me, even so send I you. And when He had said this He breathed on them, and saith unto them, Receive ye the Holy Ghost: whose soever sins ye forgive, they are forgiven unto them: whose soever sins ye retain, they are retained."—JOHN xx. 21–23.

V

THE REMISSION OF SINS

JOHN'S account of the first day in the resurrection life of Jesus is that of an eye-witness. As we have seen in our earlier consideration, the commission which Matthew records was not uttered until nearly the end of the forty days. The story which Mark tells us is, in all probability, an account of what he had heard from Peter. Luke, in the preface to his Gospel, distinctly informs us that his writing consisted of the setting in order of facts which he had gathered together from the testimony of eye-witnesses. In this Gospel there can be no doubt that we have the account of one who was certainly present, and of one moreover, who during the life of Jesus, had entered into a most close and familiar friendship with the Lord.

His message concerning his Master was pre-eminently that of Jesus as the One through Whose mission God is manifest. The prologue of his Gospel ends with the declaration, "No man hath seen God at any time; the only-begotten Son Which is in the bosom of the Father, He hath declared Him." That is the key-word to the whole Gospel; and the words of Jesus, uttered on the first day of resurrection to the disciples gathered in the upper room, which supremely impressed John, were those which harmonised most perfectly with his consistent presentation of Jesus as the Word of God, the Manifester of the Father, the Son of God.

He tells how, when Jesus presenced Himself among the disciples, He greeted them by saying, "Peace be unto you," and in that greeting sought to allay their fears, as He accompanied the words with the demonstration of His identity with the One Whom they had known and loved so well, by showing them His hands and His side.

Having done this, He again uttered the same words, "Peace be unto you," but this time in view of the service to which He was about to appoint them.

On that first resurrection day the disciples were subjects of conflicting emotion. One of the evangelists describes them as having been filled with fear and great joy. Troubled, hopeful, amazed, it must have been difficult for them to believe in the reality of the things that were passing around them. Therefore the Lord, before uttering the words of His great commission, sought to bring them to clear consciousness of the fact of His resurrection. Then, to these men thus assured, He gave a charge which John records in the words which we are now to consider.

It may be that these were the first words of the commission, that the things recorded by Mark and Luke were said subsequently; or it may be that between His first greeting of peace and the last the other things were said, John recording only the words necessary to his purpose. Whether first or last in order of utterance, it will at once be agreed that this phase of the commission touches a profound note, and therefore demands careful attention. So suggestive and yet so mystical are these words of Jesus, that around them controversy has waged in the Christian Church for centuries, and there has grown up a whole ecclesiastical system which gathers its constant power over men from an interpretation of these words, upon which it bases its claims. It is not for us in the present study to discuss that system. I simply refer to it in passing in order to draw attention to the fact that whatever these words may mean, they were spoken not to the apostles alone, but to the whole company of believers gathered together in the upper room.

As a matter of fact, in these words we have one phase of the charge of the risen Lord to His disciples as to their responsibility concerning the world; and in them we find a new note, a different emphasis, a fresh phase of suggestion. We have heard Him command us to proclaim Him King. We have heard Him call us to go into the midst of suffering creation in order to heal it. We have heard Him declare that we are to be His witnesses, His revelations. Now we hear Him charge us that we are to go to the world empowered to forgive or to retain sins.

The command in its simplicity, as it would appear to one who had never heard it expounded, or who had no prejudice concerning it, is a most startling one, demanding most earnest attention.

We shall again follow the same method of consideration as in our former studies, inquiring what is the deposit committed to the Church; what therefore, is the debt which the Church owes her Lord and the world in the presence of the deposit; and finally, what is the dynamic by which she is equipped for the discharge of her debt? These three divisions are most clearly manifest, although they do not follow that order.

Let us first then, note them as they occur. The Church's debt is indicated in the first words of the passage, "As the Father hath sent Me, even so send I you." The dynamic in which she is able to fulfil her mission is revealed in the words of Jesus, "Receive ye the Holy Ghost." The deposit committed to her is revealed in the final words, "Whose soever sins ye forgive, they are forgiven unto them; whose soever sins ye retain, they are retained." Following the order of previous considerations, we will first consider that deposit.

Before considering the authority vested in the disciples, as indicated in these words, let us notice the suggested alternative: sins forgiven, sins unforgiven. The Authorised Version reads here, "Whose soever sins ye remit, they are remitted unto them; and whose soever sins ye retain, they are retained." In this instance I prefer the Authorised translation, for the simple reason that for English readers the two words, *remit* and *retain*, stand more evidently and clearly in antithesis.

The word translated "forgive" has as its root and essential meaning exactly what is indicated in the word "remit." Forgiveness is not the passing over of wrong done, with the understanding that it is never to be mentioned. That is not the New Testament idea of forgiveness. The root idea of the word must be borne in mind. It is that of setting free from, creating liberty with regard to. If my sins are forgiven, I am set free from them, and from all the consequences following upon them. Forgiveness of sins is not merely the decision of God that He will not punish man for them. The remission of penalty is an effect resulting from a cause, and the cause is the remission of the sin. Forgiveness means that the sinner is set free from sins as to their guilt, their power, their presence.

It may be immediately objected that such definition includes in forgiveness the experience of sanctification; and this is perfectly true. Sanctification is potentially included in justification; and the forgiveness of sins in the economy of God includes the setting free of the sinner from the sins themselves, and therefore from their consequences of every description.

The forgiveness of sins always results in two things: first in a new vision of God;

and secondly, and consequently, in a new motive of life. That fact is demonstrated by the experience of the saints as revealed in the New Testament, and as revealed in all subsequent history. In that moment in which the soul comes to the consciousness that sins are forgiven, there dawns upon it a conception of God which is entirely new. The word of Isaiah is of perpetual application; "Your iniquities have separated between you and your God, and your sins have hid His face from you." In the moment in which a man is set free from his sins this separation ends, and the face of God is seen.

That new vision, following upon the consciousness of sin forgiven, becomes the new motive of life, the secret of holiness, the impulse of compassion, the reason of activity. The new vision is that of God as love; which, producing love to God, makes love for evermore the motive of life.

The forgiveness of sins is the fundamental note in the evangel which the Church proclaims to the world in the name of the crucified and risen Christ. No other form of religion offers it to man. As we have constantly affirmed, there is a measure of light in every form of religion, from that of the fetish worship of the savage to that of the teaching of Buddha; but no religion approaches man with the declaration that seeing he is unable to walk in the light, it brings to him a forgiveness of sins which means moral reconstruction; so that from henceforth he may walk therein, in the strength and beauty of holiness. The risen Lord declared to His disciples that He sent them to the world, empowered to forgive sins.

This includes however, that which is its opposite, namely, the retention of sins. If forgiveness means freedom from sins, retention means slavery to sin. The man whose sins are retained is not loosed from them, but bound by them. Such a man has no vision of God, and therefore his motive of life is a false motive, and consequently all his life is a false life.

As a matter of fact, in one of these two conditions all men who have heard the Evangel are living at this moment. There are those whose sins are remitted, and those whose sins are retained. Or, to state the antithesis in the terms of result, there are men and women who have seen God so as to love Him and so as to serve Him; and men and women who, lacking the vision of God, are afraid of Him, and are at enmity against Him. Or, once again to state the division in terms of the final issue, there are men and women whose motive in life is to do the will of God, and men and women whose motive is to please themselves.

According to this charge of Christ, His disciples are sent with a message, by which there is created for men a crisis of choice; and when men make their choice, as they are compelled to do who hear the Word, the disciples, with their Lord's authority, which is the authority of heaven and eternity and of final destiny, pronounce the verdict of sins remitted, or of sins retained, according to the choice which men make.

In the proclamation of the Kingship and Saviourhood of the Lord Jesus Christ, men are inevitably brought to a crisis. The question of Pilate is the question of every man who confronts Christ, "What then shall I do with Jesus?" One man answers, repenting; I trust Him. To that man the commissioned disciple declares; Thy sins, which are many, are remitted. Another man replies; Crucify Him. To that man the message of the commissioned disciple is; Thy sins are retained.

This is our fundamental message. We are not sent to men to discuss with them the relative values of their religions. In our going to them we must respect the light which they already possess, and attempt to lead them toward the fuller light; but our supreme business is to preach Christ crucified and risen, thereby to compel men to stand in the presence of His Saviourhood, and make their choice; and upon the basis of that choice we are charged to remit or retain sins, according to whether they crown or crucify Him.

Ere we leave this statement of the deposit it is necessary that we should recognise the conditions which are involved in our Lord's method of stating it. For the purpose of our study we have commenced at the end of the passage, but we cannot commence there in our service. Let us emphasise the sequence revealed by tabulation of the threefold declaration :—

"As the Father hath sent Me, even so send I you."

"Receive ye the Holy Ghost."

"Whose soever sins ye forgive, they are forgiven unto them ; whose soever sins ye retain, they are retained."

If we attempt to remit or retain sins save in that line of succession, we are guilty of the worst blasphemy possible.

The whole movement begins with God; "As the Father hath sent Me." It proceeds through the Son; the Son is the Sent of the Father. It is carried forward by the ministry of the Spirit; "Receive ye the Holy Ghost." It is accomplished through the instrumentality of men and women indwelt by the Spirit, given by the Son, received from the Father.

The final authority for forgiving sins does not rest with men or women, but with God; and He exercises His authority through the mediation of the Son, and the administration of the Spirit, through the members of the Church. Only thus can we forgive or retain sin. Words of absolution are utterly useless save as they are spoken in the power of the indwelling Spirit, in fellowship with the crucified and crowned Christ, and under the authority of the living God. Words of absolution or sentence of retention can only be uttered; therefore, upon the fulfilment of the conditions declared by Christ Himself.

Thus in the upper room, on the first day of resurrection, suggestively and prophetically our Lord recognised the union of His disciples with Himself, and therefore with the Father; and upon the basis of that union He sent them forth to the exercise of this high and awful prerogative.

This is the fundamental note in the commission of the Christian Church. Whether it be in England, in China, or in India; in city or village or hamlet; to bond or free, to rich or poor, to learned or illiterate; we take to men a Saviour in Whose presence they make a choice which results either in the remission or retention of their sins; and we are authorised to remit or retain according to what their choice shall be.

From this consideration we pass necessarily and naturally to a consideration of our debt, as indicated in the words of the Lord; "As the Father has sent Me, even so send I you."

It is evident that the key to the interpretation of these words is found in the two words which suggest the comparison, "As . . . so." To see and understand the work of the Son as the Sent of the Father is to see and understand the debt we owe to the world, as those sent by the Son. Our first inquiry then, must be as to the purpose of His sending; and, in order to a satisfactory answer to the inquiry, the whole Gospel of John is needed. All that it contains however, for purposes of the present study, may be suggested by the use of two simple words; the Father sent the Son for Manifestation and for Co-operation. The whole truth is contained potentially in that master-declaration at the close of the prologue to which we have already referred: "No man hath seen God at any time: the only-begotten Son, Which is in the bosom of the Father, He hath declared Him." His declaration of the Father consisted in Manifestation and Co-operation.

When at the close of His ministry the Lord gave His disciples final instruction in what we speak of as the Paschal discourses, Philip suddenly exclaimed; "Show us the Father, and it sufficeth us." In those words essential humanity uttered its deepest need. All the unrest of to-day, east and west, north and south, is but the expression of the same need. To that cry Christ answered "He that hath seen Me hath seen the Father." He was sent of the Father that men through Him might see the Father. John, His familiar friend, the one who perhaps more intently than any of the other disciples, had gazed upon Him, and more often than any other, had handled Him, declared; "We beheld His glory—glory as of the only-begotten from the Father, full of grace and truth. These are comprehensive, inclusive, exhaustive words. The Father sent the Son for manifestation. He came, and in Him men saw Grace and Truth.

It is most important that in the recitation of the passage, "The law was given by Moses; grace and truth came by Jesus Christ," we should not employ an emphasis which denies its essential meaning. We are in the habit of reading the declaration as though the law that came by Moses was characterised by severity only, while the grace and truth that came by Jesus Christ were characterised by tenderness only. As a matter of fact, the law of Moses was the expression of love, and it must not be forgotten that truth is a more awful word than law. Law is but the expression of truth in certain applications to individual needs. Truth is essential, eternal, unswerving, unbending. Not grace only, but truth also came by Christ. These were the supreme facts in the manifestation, for which the Son of God was sent.

He came not for manifestation only, but also for co-operation. And here again we may take one illustration from the Gospel of John, this time from the beginning of

His ministry rather than from the close. After He had healed the man in the Bethesda porches, in answer to the criticism of those who objected to His healing on the Sabbath, He said; "My Father worketh even until now, and I work." The importance of that declaration may be gathered from the fact that on the human side that claim cost Christ His life. From the moment of its utterance His enemies sought opportunity to kill Him; and if John's grouping of facts be carefully studied, it will be discovered that the claim which He then made was that to which His enemies most profoundly objected, and for which at last they crucified Him.

It was indeed a great word; "My Father worketh even until now, and I work." I think its simplest and sublimest interpretation is discovered by turning from all speculation, and considering it in the light of the actual miracle which gave rise to it. When His enemies charged Him with breaking Sabbath in healing this man, He used these words, and if I may attempt most reverently to interpret His meaning by expressing the thought in other words, it is as though He had said; You charge Me with breaking Sabbath because I have healed this man. Do you not know and understand that God has never had a Sabbath since man sinned? "My Father worketh." Man broke in upon the rest of God when he sinned; and God can never be at rest while humanity sins and suffers. It was a declaration that in the presence of human sin, God is active instead of passive; and moreover, that His activity is in order to restore rest to those who have lost it.

To this declaration He added the significant words, "and I work," thus claiming co-operation with God, which co-operation was illustrated in what He had then done. The suffering man had been without Sabbath for eight-and-thirty years, and by his healing had been restored to the possibility of rest. In order to accomplish this, Christ, in fellowship with God, had lost His rest. This then, is the revelation of the debt we owe to the world. As the Father sent the Son, so the Son sends us, for manifestation and for co-operation.

This conception of our debt is one calculated to inspire us with the loftiest ambition, and at the same time to humble us to the dust in shame. Every disciple of Jesus ought to be able to look into the face of those hot and restless souls who lack the vision of God because of sin, and say; He that hath seen me hath seen the Christ; my Saviour worketh even until now, and I work. It is impossible to say this without an overwhelming sense of shame filling the soul on account of failure and shortcoming.

And yet let us carefully conceive the great ideal. The Church is sent to the world for the manifestation of the Manifester. The Church is sent to the world for co-operation with the Son, Who co-operates with the Father, in order to set it free from all the bonds that bind it. It ought to be that wherever humanity is hot and restless for lack of God, humanity can find God in the people of God.

Our debt to the world is that of revealing Christ to men, and of working in fellowship with Christ. To fulfil this responsibility is to be for ever restless in the presence of human restlessness, to abandon all our personal rights and privileges and Sabbaths, in order that we may toil and thus create Sabbath for others. "As the Father hath sent Me, even so send I you."

Wherever the disciples co-operate thus with Christ in manifestation, they produce a crisis in human lives, bringing men to the point where they must choose. Whenever the disciples co-operate thus with Christ in service, they have the right to pronounce the remitting or retaining word, according to the decision that men make in the hour of crisis.

This is a most solemn consideration, and we do well honestly to face it, however much such action may rebuke us, in order that by new dedication of all we are to Him we may enter into the realisation of His great purpose. We cannot live in fellowship with Christ without compelling those with whom we come in contact to stand face to face with Him. And whenever we do this, and they are thus brought to the crisis of choice, it is our business to declare to them the way of the life we live, and when in response to that declaration they receive or reject Him, we are authorised to declare their sins remitted or retained.

And finally, in the great central word of the passage, our Lord clearly reveals the dynamic; and in the light of the solemnity of the work committed to us, how conscious we are of our need of that which He promised to His disciples. If in very deed the tremendous responsibility rests upon us, as Christian men and women, of bringing the world to the crisis of choice, in order that sins may be remitted or retained; we are inevitably compelled to exclaim, "Who is sufficient for these things?"

The answer to that necessary inquiry is contained in the action and the words of Christ as here recorded. He prophetically breathed upon that first group of disciples, and said to them, "Receive ye the Holy Ghost." I use the word "prophetically, because they did not then receive the Spirit for on that same occasion in the upper room, as Luke records, He charged His disciples to tarry in the city until they were clothed with power from on high. His action of breathing upon them indicated the fact that the Spirit could only be bestowed upon them in fulness through Him; and His word indicated the fact that it was only possible for them to fulfil their responsibility in the power of the Spirit.

It is of supreme importance here that we should connect this word with the comparison which we have already considered. That may be done perhaps by reading the words that He uttered, omitting for a moment the declaration of the prophetic breathing. "*As* the Father hath sent Me, even *so* send I you. . . . Receive *ye* the Holy Spirit." The suggestion of these words is that Jesus fulfilled His mission in co-operation with the Spirit, and that we through Him have the same Spirit at our disposal for the doing of our work, as He had for the doing of His. If we think again of the story of His mission of manifestation and co-operation, it may be told in very brief chapters. He was born of the Spirit; He was anointed by the Spirit; He exercised His ministry in the power of the Spirit; He offered Himself to God upon the Cross through the eternal

Spirit. Even after His resurrection, according to the words of Luke in the book of the Acts, He gave commandment to the apostles through the Holy Ghost.

The whole ministry of Jesus was a ministry of fellowship with the Spirit. The Father gave the Spirit to Him, the eternal Son, not by measure, but in fulness. If that be remembered, there is new force in the words, "*As* the Father hath sent Me, even *so* send I you . . . receive *ye* the Holy Ghost." The men and women who are commissioned by Christ to remit or retain sins are those who have spiritual union with Christ in the most absolute sense of the word.

He was born of the Spirit; so also is the believer. It may be objected that there is a very great difference, and yet does the objection hold good? Is it not true that the life which we now live is a life which began when we were born of the Spirit? All that which preceded the hour of the new birth is cancelled, has ceased to be. The things that were gain are counted but dung and dross. We have sometimes smiled when we have heard some illiterate man declare on a given day that it was his birthday, and that he was three, or seven, or ten years of age, when apparently he was a man of forty or fifty, or more. And yet he was perfectly right. He began to live when he was born of the Spirit of God. It is only such as live this new life which had its beginning by the action of the Spirit of God, who can possibly manifest Christ or co-operate with Him.

Again, He was anointed by the Spirit; and so also is the believer; and in that anointing perfect equipment is provided for all the work to be done.

He exercised His ministry in the power of the Spirit; and the same power is perpetually at the disposal of all those whom He sends, both for the perfecting of the life for manifestation, and its empowering for co-operation.

And finally, as through the eternal Spirit, He offered Himself to God; the bestowment of the Spirit upon the believer is not only for new manhood and new equipment, but also for new suffering. No man can tell another that his sins are forgiven, unless in some measure he knows what it is to have fellowship with the suffering of Christ. It is only when we are swayed and swept by the compassion of Jesus, and only when we can say, "I could wish that I myself were anathema from Christ for my brethren's sake," that we have power to pronounce the word of absolution.

If on account of our own feebleness of realisation these things are stated negatively, it is well for us to remember that this word of Jesus, and the work which followed it, mean that the Spirit is at the disposal of the believer for life, for work, and for suffering; and therein is created both the authority and the power by which we are sent to men in order that they may be brought to remission or retention of sins.

Thus inclusively in the power of the Spirit we can manifest the Christ and co-operate with Him. This great power for the proclamation of the evangel, for the creation of the crisis, for the pronunciation of remission or retention is not vested in a few, but in the whole Church; and she is able to exercise that power in proportion as she is abandoned to the dominion of the Spirit, and thus is living the life of fellowship with the Lord.

This then, is the fundamental message of the Christian evangel, and this the great offer of God to men, which the Church is responsible for making. She is commissioned to go to all men and tell them that through Christ it is possible that their sins may be forgiven; that they may have a new moral beginning in spiritual power.

When Nicodemus said unto Jesus, "How can a man be born when he is old? Can he enter a second time into his mother's womb, and be born?" his question was not flippant as some people seem to imagine. He meant, What can a man do with the days already lived? How can the nature which he received at the beginning be changed? The answer of Christ was, and is, that it is possible for a man to be born anew of the Spirit; that in that new birth there is moral regeneration; that in that moral regeneration life begins again, equipped for reconstruction.

That is the message of the Church to the

world, and that pulpit disastrously fails, and that missionary endeavour lacks its supreme note, where this evangel is not proclaimed and this authority is not exercised. It is for this moreover, that the world is supremely waiting. Humanity is one, the round world over; and whether men be struggling, or hoping to struggle, through long processes to reach the obliteration of personality that blots out sin, or whether men are crying in still more acute agony, "What must we do to be saved?" the supreme and underlying need is that of the remission of sins. Our business in the world is to bring men to Christ, and so to the possibility of such remission.

By the world's need, by the Christ's compassion, by the desire and purpose of God, by the hope of the salvation of our own lives, if we name His name we must carry His burden and fulfil His purpose. As the Father sent Him, and He sends us, so must we go, bearing to men in the power of the Spirit the glad news of the possibility of sins forgiven and peace with heaven.

THE FOURFOLD RESOURCE AND RESPONSIBILITY

“*Take My yoke upon you.*”—MATTHEW xi. 29.

“*He shall be servant of all.*”—MARK x. 44.

“*Tarry ye in the city, until ye be clothed with power from on high.*”—LUKE xxiv. 49.

“*Abide in Me.*”—JOHN xv. 3.

VI

THE FOURFOLD RESOURCE AND RESPONSIBILITY

IN the light of the matters already considered, our last study must necessarily be personal, and have to do with the conditions upon which it is possible to avail ourselves of the resources at our disposal for the fulfilment of our responsibilities.

In order to clearness of apprehension, let us first re-state the teaching of the Gospels as to our responsibilities and resources.

First then, as to our responsibilities. These are created by our deposit.

The Gospel according to Matthew is the Gospel of the King. The commission of Jesus as there recorded charges us to declare His regal authority.

The Gospel according to Mark is the Gospel

of the Servant of God. The commission of Jesus as there recorded lays upon us the responsibility of proclaiming in the kosmos the good news of His renewing ministry.

The Gospel according to Luke is the Gospel of the perfect and perfecting Man. The commission of Jesus as there recorded makes us responsible for revealing His redeeming ability.

The Gospel according to John is the Gospel of the manifestation of God. The commission of Jesus as there recorded calls us to co-operation with Him in the great ministry for the remission of sins.

To summarise yet more briefly, the missionary deposit which the Church possesses for the world is that of the regal authority, the renewing ministry, the redeeming ability, and the reconciling work of the Son of God.

Our debt in each case is conditioned by the deposit. We are to proclaim His royalty, we are to have fellowship with Him in His renewing ministry, we are to demonstrate in our own lives His redeeming ability, and we are to co-operate with Him in His reconciling work.

As to our resources, these are declared in each case, side by side with the declarations of responsibility.

When Jesus charged His first disciples to disciple the nations, He said, "I am with you alway." The presence of the King constitutes the power for proclaiming His royalty.

When He charged them to go into the kosmos and to preach the evangel to the whole creation, it is written immediately that they went forth, "the Lord working with them." Power for the fulfilment of this phase of responsibility is that of His fellowship with us in suffering, in sacrifice, and so in healing ministry.

When He charged them that they were to be His witnesses, He promised them the Holy Spirit, and on the day of Pentecost fulfilled His promise. Power for such witness is that of the indwelling and transforming Spirit.

When He charged them to remit or retain sins, He did so in conjunction with the declaration that He sent them as the Father had sent Him. Power for this most sacred work is provided in that vital union of believers with Himself, which is most perfectly set forth under His own matchless figure of the vine.

Thus it is at once seen that all our resources for fulfilling the ministry are in Him. If we are to proclaim His royalty; if we are to have fellowship with His suffering ministry of renewal; if we are to manifest His redeeming ability; if we are to be in true co-operation with Him in the manifestation of God, and the putting away of sin; we must avail ourselves of the resources which He has provided.

This brings us to our present inquiry. Upon what conditions can we appropriate the promises of power which He made, in order to the discharge of the debt created by the deposit in each case?

Let us ask the questions separately. How may I enter into such consciousness of the presence of the King as to be able to proclaim His royalty? How may I enter into such fellowship with the actual suffering Servant of God as to be able to communicate His healing power to the creation? How may

I enter into such true realisation of all the powers of His life as to demonstrate in the world His redeeming ability? How may I have His life so flowing through my own that through me God may be manifested for the putting away of sins?

These conditions may be stated in each case by quotation of supreme and central words peculiar to the gospel which reveals the phase of missionary responsibility under consideration.

At this point we must draw the necessary distinction between responsibility for the proclamation of the evangel, and responsibility as to our ability to proclaim. We have spoken of our responsibility to the world, but how are we to fulfil it? It is already conceded that our resources are in Christ, but how are we to avail ourselves of these resources?

In order to the proclamation of the royalty of Jesus there is a simple and all-inclusive condition. It is to be found in one simple, brief, and in some senses incomplete quotation from the eleventh chapter of Matthew, "Take My yoke upon you." In order that we may gather the force of this word, we must consider it in its contextual light.

The closing paragraph of that chapter contains the supreme call and claim of the King. It is the most significant and stupendous claim that Jesus ever uttered. It is well that we should have it before us in its entirety.

"All things have been delivered unto Me of My Father: and no one knoweth the Son, save the Father; neither doth any know the Father save the Son, and he to whomsoever the Son willeth to reveal Him. Come unto Me, all ye that labour and are heavy laden, and I will give you rest. Take My yoke upon you, and learn of Me; for I am meek and lowly in heart: and ye shall find rest unto your souls."

If in a brief word I may attempt to express the meaning of the great passage, I shall do so by saying that Christ therein affirmed that all the restlessness of humanity is due to the anarchy of humanity; to the fact that man is not living his life in relation to the government and authority of God.

He claimed that God had given Him all authority to reveal Him to men. He claimed that man can only find his way into rest as he comes into the government of God; and that he can only find his way into that government through Himself. In view of these facts His call was threefold; first, "Come unto Me"; secondly, "Take My yoke"; finally, "Learn of Me."

Out of the centre of that sublime passage, with its supreme claim and call, I take that word "Take My yoke upon you," as revealing the one and only condition, upon fulfilment of which, we shall be able to proclaim His royalty. I am perfectly familiar with the fact that the word has many wide and spacious applications with which I am not now proposing to deal. I take the simplest only. Loyalty is the condition for the victorious proclamation of royalty. If the Church of God is to proclaim in power the fact of the Lordship of Christ, she must herself be loyal to Him, taking His yoke upon her.

There is a fact full of encouragement, not to be forgotten in this connection.

When Jesus said, "Take My yoke upon you," He spoke in the first place not of the yoke He was imposing upon others, but of the yoke He Himself wore as Man. That was the yoke of a perfect surrender to the will of God, and absolute submission to His throne. To all who come to Him He says, "Take My yoke; the yoke I wear is the yoke I impose upon you. As I am submissive to government, so also must you be, if you are to exercise authority." Said the Roman centurion, "I also am a man under authority, having under myself soldiers." The condition for the exercise of authority is ever that of submission to authority.

Therein consists the whole philosophy of our responsibility. If we are to proclaim the royalty of Jesus we must wear His yoke and yield ourselves to His Kingship. The secret of power for the declaration of the Kingship of Jesus in the world, and for the bringing of the world to the consciousness of that Kingship, is that of the realisation within ourselves of all the meaning of His government. This will issue in the manifestation to the world of the breadth and beneficence of that government. In the power of such realisation and manifestation, there may be such insistence upon His Kingship as will issue in triumph.

The Church of God will never make the world believe that Jesus is in very deed and truth the King until she is herself submitted to His Kingship. I suppose that statement may raise some measure of resentment. I may be asked if I mean to suggest that the Church of God is not loyal to the Kingship of Christ? I mean more than to suggest it; I declare that it is so; and I affirm that to be the reason of all her weakness and failure.

We regularly pray, until sometimes one is almost afraid of the formalism of it, "Thy Kingdom come, Thy will be done." That prayer prevails in the measure in which we ourselves hallow the name, are submitted to the Kingship, and do the will of God. Our work in the world prevails in the proportion in which we are loyal to the Lord Christ. My heart is full of hope and full of expectation when I look out over the world, for everywhere there are evidences of the activity of the Spirit of God. The only hour in which I am depressed is that in which I look within the Christian Church. Do we believe in His Lordship? Do we believe He is King? Let the question be answered individually and privately and honestly, only let us remember that we cannot make the world believe that we believe, save as we are loyal to His Kingship. Unless we are so submitted to Him that there is manifest to the world the gracious influence of that submission, we have no prevailing argument for His Kingship. The breadth and the glory and the beauty, resulting from our own submission to the Kingship of Jesus, must be our argument as we proclaim His royalty to the world.

The condition upon which we may avail ourselves of the resources provided for the fulfilment of the second phase of commission is indicated in the words, "Servant of all." Again let us gather the contextual light upon that imperfect phrase.

James and John, the sons of Zebedee,

asked the Lord that they might sit, one on His right hand, and the other on His left, in His Kingdom. When we are inclined to be angry with them let us remember how infinitely tender Jesus was. He rebuked them; but in great tenderness and great patience He said, "Ye know not what ye ask. Are ye able to drink the cup that I drink? or to be baptized with the baptism that I am baptized with?" And they said, "We are able." They meant it. They were absolutely honest, but they were appallingly ignorant. Then with a great foreseeing of His own method of fulfilment He said, "The cup that I drink ye shall drink; and with the baptism that I am baptized withal shall ye be baptized." He then went on to teach them that the underlying purpose of their inquiry was wrong. "It is not Mine," He said, "to give this right to sit on My right hand to any except to those for whom it is prepared." Moreover, their request for the place of power made it evident that they had not yet come to fellowship with His cup and baptism. Then it was that He said, "Whosoever would be first among you, shall be *servant of all"*; and He illuminated His meaning and inspired them to humility by the great declaration, "The Son of Man came not to be ministered unto, but to minister, and to give His life a ransom for many."

The teaching as to responsibility is that in order to fellowship with Jesus in His renewing ministry, the selfless motive of activity is necessary. "Servant of all"; and the word must be interpreted by His declaration concerning Himself that He came "not to be ministered unto but to minister." I do not think that this application can be made in the midst of a multitude. It must be made alone. It must be made quietly. Let us seek to discover the principle, and then leave the matter. The principle is that in order to fellowship with Jesus in the proclamation of the evangel to the whole creation, we must be at the end of that subtly selfish motive which is so slow to die. A question which ought to be asked by every disciple at work for the Master is the question, Why? Why am I doing this? What am I seeking? My own enrichment, my fame, my comfort, my ease? I repeat, these questions are not for public answer. They are for private examination, and they must be faced. So long as there lurks in our service, even though we know that service to be of the highest and the best in its intention and purpose, the desire that somehow or other it may serve us and minister to us, we have not come into true fellowship with Christ. He came not to be ministered unto. He did not seek anything for Himself. For evermore He was unmindful of Himself. He was mindful of the things of others, and the whole truth may again be revealed by a quotation, quite apart from the context. I call His own enemies, from the midst of ribald mockery, into the witness-box, and quite unintentionally they tell the whole story of the Servant of God. "He saved others, Himself He cannot save." I propose to amend the declaration, and to declare that He saved others, Himself He did not seek to save, or desire to save, or attempt to save; and therein is revealed the whole secret of fellowship with Him in renewing and healing work. Our service must have at its centre nothing of self-seeking. That is a matter, I repeat for the third time, not now to be applied, but to be faced when we are alone.

Let us pass then, to the third phase of the commission—that namely, of the demonstration of redeeming ability. How are we to appropriate the resources of His life, so that through our lives witness may be borne to His power? Here we turn to the actual words of the commission, because therein Christ so clearly indicated the conditions upon which we shall be able to fulfil this ministry of witness. He commanded those first disciples in Jerusalem, "Tarry ye in the city, until ye be clothed with power from on high."

Nothing in ourselves of wisdom, or of planning, or of power, or of endeavour is sufficient to the demonstration before the eyes of men of the redeeming ability of Christ. We cannot be witnesses in the full and gracious and glorious sense of the word by any strength or wisdom of our own. Dealing with the commission, we carefully drew attention to a matter which it is of the utmost importance that we consider again. The principle involved in the command to tarry is an abiding principle. It is that we are not equal to witness in our own power. We need the power of the Holy Spirit. The application is changed. The disciples had to wait for fifty days for the coming of the Spirit; for the forty during which the Lord remained among them, and for the ten during which He was absent and they were waiting in the upper room. We have not to wait half an hour for the Spirit of God. The Spirit has been given, and is immediately at the disposal of all believers for fulfilment of their responsibility.

The abiding principle is that the Church, in order to bear her witness, must depend wholly and absolutely on the Spirit. Such dependence is the condition of realisation, and consequently the condition of manifestation. We supremely need to recognise this truth in its application to the corporate life and testimony of the Church. We cannot bear witness to the redeeming ability of Christ in our Church life in any other way than that of ceasing to put our trust in men; ceasing to seek help from men; ceasing to employ the methods which are carnal and worldly-wise; and abandoning ourselves utterly and wholly to the life and the light and the love of the Holy Spirit of God.

The principle has also the most immediate personal application. If we attempt to teach in the Sunday School in any other power than that of our dependence on the Spirit, we are doomed to failure. If we attempt to preach in any other way than that of dependence on the Spirit, we are foreordained to failure. If we attempt to evangelise the heathen by our own cleverness, by our own new methods, apart from the power of the Spirit, our efforts are entirely useless.

All this becomes the more searching and solemn a consideration as we remember that if we tarry, blame attaches to us, because there need be no tarrying. We can take our way, if we will, to our work in the school, endued with power from on high. We can go to our pulpits, if we will, in the fulness of the Holy Spirit. We can proceed to the uttermost part of the earth, if we will, in the power and demonstration of the Spirit; for the Spirit has been given and never withdrawn.

Nevertheless the principle must not be forgotten. Unless we have this enduement, unless we are in conscious fellowship with the Spirit of God, we cannot bear witness to the world of the redeeming ability of the Christ.

Now we come to the last phase of the commission, which in some senses is the most wonderful and most awe-inspiring of them all. What is the abiding condition of co-operation with Christ in the reconciling work of revealing the Father and of dealing with the sins of men? The answer is fully given in the word of our Lord, "Abide in Me." Again we need the contextual light, and must recall the teaching of that wonderful fifteenth chapter of the Gospel of John.

Occurring in the midst of the discourses which Jesus uttered to His disciples before

He left them, it constitutes a commentary on the union between Himself and them which would follow His death, resurrection, ascension, and the coming of the Spirit. We must think of the whole figure, in order to make application of the condition enjoined by the words, "Abide in Me." That whole figure is contained in the words of Christ, "I am the Vine." Unless we are careful, we miss the force and beauty of the teaching suggested in these words. I fear that we are in the habit of reading the passage as though Christ had said, I am the main stem of the vine, and you are the branches; whereas His word was far more remarkable. He said, "I am the Vine." That is inclusive; root, and stem, and branches, and leaves, and tendrils, and clusters of fruit. The vine is not complete without its branches, and we at once see that what is suggested is, that the branches are a veritable part of Himself; that while it is true, most solemnly true, that apart from Him—that is, severed from Him—branches can do nothing, it is equally true that apart from the branches He cannot bear fruit. He is dependent on the branches, as the branches are dependent upon Him. That is the fact which creates the solemnity of our responsibility.

The awe-inspiring note of this responsibility creates our anxiety as to the conditions upon which we may avail ourselves of those resources which are necessary to fulfilment. Our resources are all in Him. His life unhindered must issue in the fruit which glorifies God, being produced in the branches.

What then, is the teaching as to conditions? Manifestation and co-operation are only possible by maintained identification, "Abide in Me." To deal with sins for remission or retention we must abide in Him; to be able to bring to men that unveiling of God which produces conviction and provides deliverance, we must abide in Him.

Such consideration makes the word "abide" almost appalling in its solemnity. We recognise the absolute necessity for abiding in Him. We see how the branch perishes and is only fit for burning, when severed from Him, and we are filled with fear. The word is severe with a terrible severity, revealing to us our utter helplessness in the presence of our responsibility, and bowing us to the dust with the consciousness thereof.

But the word thrills with a great tenderness also, and is characterised by a gracious simplicity. There are one or two of the very simplest matters we need to remember. These words were words spoken to the men who knew Him intimately after the flesh. We must remember however, that they were spoken to simple, trembling, troubled hearts, like our own. The one condition of abiding is weakness. It does not require any effort to abide. We enter a building, and for a period we abide in that building without effort. We make effort when we leave it. Abiding therefore, is a word which indicates weakness, and the consciousness of it; and the yielding to it, so that weakness is the strength which keeps us in Christ.

Abiding in Christ makes no intellectual demand upon us. We are not always equally conscious that we are in Him. We have said on the morning of some given day, that for the day we would abide in Christ, we would never forget Him, we would keep Him in mind; but we have never succeeded. We start into the business of the day; into the midst of the city with its rush and its roar; into the following of our necessary and proper vocation; and soon, so far as our immediate consciousness is concerned, we have forgotten Him; and then the heart is troubled. But it need not be; we abide in Him, even though we are not conscious of Him. To return to the simple figure already used, we enter a building and remain in it. We do not remember all the time that we are in the building, but we abide there. So abiding in Christ is not the result of strength; neither is it dependent upon constant consciousness of the fact.

What then, is it to abide in Him? He did not leave us without clear instruction, for He said, "He that keepeth My commandments abideth in Me." To abide then, is to obey. To obey is to abide. If we would abide in Him, we are quietly to obey Him; and if we do so, then we abide in Him.

And if we do so, then abiding in Him, all the tides of His life flow through us, and produce the fruit which is to the glory of God.

What the Church supremely needs in order to the revelation of the Father for the reconciliation of men by the remission of their sins, is abounding life; and the Church can only have abounding life as she abides in her Lord, in quiet and restful but determined obedience, to whatever He may say to her.

In conclusion, by contrast we discover the reasons of failure. A divided heart toward the King hinders the coming of the Kingdom Self uncrucified, so that even in the midst of toil for Christ there lurks the motive of self-enrichment, cancels the power of service and makes it useless. The using of carnal methods, either in individual life or Church work, quenches the Spirit of God, and makes all our service of no avail. Lack of abundant and abounding life prevents the manifestation of God, and makes impossible work for Him.

The cure for all such failure is the maintenance of right relation with Christ. We need a clear vision of His Kingliness, and a complete surrender thereto; a keen sense of His motive, and an answering selflessness by the way of the Cross; an abiding recognition of the perfection of His provision for us in the Holy Spirit, and a constant dependence on that Spirit for the doing of all our work; a perpetual experience of the power of His life, and an obedient abiding therein.

> "Christ for the world, we sing,
> The world to Christ we bring."

That is the whole story, but in each case those represented by the "we" must be related to Christ. We sing of Christ to the world in perfect melody and perfect harmony; and the world listens as to an ideal song. But if there enter into our singing the thrill of passion, the touch of a personal experience, then we shall not only sing of Christ to the world, but bring the world to Christ.

For the fulfilment of the Lord's missionary

commission we must be loyal to His Kingship, have fellowship in the suffering of His service, depend upon the Spirit of His gift, and abide in the full tide of His life.